SUMMER FRUIT
Pastries

SUMMER FRUIT
Pastries

60 BRIGHT AND FRESH RECIPES FOR TARTLETS,
ECLAIRS, ROULADES, PIES AND MORE

RYLAND PETERS & SMALL
LONDON • NEW YORK

Senior Designer Toni Kay
Senior Editor Abi Waters
Editorial Director Julia Charles
Creative Director Leslie Harrington
Production Manager
  Gordana Simakovic
Head of Production
  Patricia Harrington
Indexer Vanessa Bird

First published in 2023 by
Ryland Peters & Small
20–21 Jockey's Fields
London WC1R 4BW
and
341 East 116th Street
New York NY 10029
www.rylandpeters.com

Text © Valerie Aikman-Smith,
Brontë Aurell, Maxine Clark, Julian
Day, Ursula Ferrigno, Mat Follas,
Liz Franklin, Hannah Miles,
Miisa Mink, Will Torrent, Laura
Washburn Hutton, Bea Vo and
Ryland Peters & Small 2023

Design and photographs © Ryland
Peters & Small 2023

ISBN: 978-1-78879-513-5

10 9 8 7 6 5 4 3 2 1

A CIP record for this book is
available from the British Library.

US Library of Congress Cataloging-
in-Publication data has been
applied for.

Printed and bound in China

NOTES
• All spoon measurements are
level, unless otherwise specified.
• All fruit and vegetables should
be washed thoroughly before
consumption. Unwaxed citrus fruits
should be used whenever possible.
• The recipes in this book are
given in both metric and imperial
measurements. However, the
spellings are primarily British.
• All eggs are medium (UK) or
large (US), unless specified as
large, in which case US extra-large
should be used. Uncooked or
partially cooked eggs should not
be served to the very old, frail,
young children, pregnant women
or those with compromised
immune systems.
• Ovens should be preheated
to the specified temperatures. If
using a fan-assisted oven, adjust
temperatures according to the
manufacturer's instructions.
• When a recipe calls for the
grated zest of citrus fruit, buy
unwaxed fruit and wash well
before using.

MIX
Paper | Supporting
responsible forestry
FSC® C008047

Contents

Introduction

Bright summer days and warm, balmy evenings evoke thoughts of entertaining and enjoying delicious food at leisure with family and friends – picnics, parties, barbecues/cookouts and beautiful spreads of tasty summer feasts – and these events are never without a bountiful selection of irresistible desserts.

Flaky, buttery pastry is the perfect complement to sharp and sweet summer fruits and this wonderful combination works beautifully as a sun-drenched dessert or sweet treat, whether it be a tiny, bite-sized pastry bite that will satisfy those sweet, fruity cravings, or a larger fruit-filled tart or pie to feed a crowd.

Pies and heavy pastry desserts are often associated with the colder months in the year, but here they are given a summery makeover by pairing them with the wonderful bounty of summer fruits that exist. Sun-kissed berries, zesty lemons and limes, tangy rhubarb and juicy peaches all appear in this selection of fruity recipes.

Fruit-forward tarts and pies are also joined by an array of choux and puff pastry desserts, from profiteroles to eclairs and millefeuilles to free-form pies.

This impressive collection is rounded off by a small selection of other summery desserts as they were just too good not to include – delectable roulades, biscuit/cookie-based pies and other easy breezy desserts all filled with the vibrant flavours of summer.

The recipes really do cover all the bases with some recipes using shop-bought pastry to satisfy those immediate or last-minute needs, or for when you just don't have much time to spare; and others include recipes for homemade pastry for when you want to enjoy some time in the kitchen and cook up a feast.

We hope you enjoy this sunshine recipe collection and find a pastry delight to suit any summer desire or occasion.

BITE-SIZED TREATS

Raspberry & rose tartlets

PASTRY
60 g/½ stick butter, chilled and diced
140 g/1 cup plain/ all-purpose flour, sifted, plus extra for dusting
a pinch of salt

CRÈME PÂTISSIÈRE
1 tablespoon cornflour/ cornstarch
1 tablespoon rosewater
60 g/⅓ cup caster/ superfine sugar
1 egg and 1 egg yolk
100 ml/scant ½ cup full-fat/whole milk
150 ml/⅔ cup double/ heavy cream

TO ASSEMBLE
50 g/⅓ cup chopped dark/ bittersweet chocolate, melted
250 g/2 cups raspberries
chopped pistachios

GLAZE
3 tablespoons apricot glaze

12-hole fluted muffin pan, greased
9-cm/3½-in. round cookie cutter
piping/pastry bag fitted with large star nozzle/tip

MAKES 12

These dainty pies are perfect to serve for a summery afternoon tea. The tart cases are lined with a thin layer of dark/bittersweet chocolate, which offers the perfect foil to the sharpness of the fruit.

For the pastry, rub the butter into the flour and salt using your fingertips. Add 1 tablespoon of cold water and mix in with a round-bladed knife, adding a little more water if the mixture is too dry. Wrap the pastry in clingfilm/plastic wrap and chill in the refrigerator for 1 hour.

On a flour-dusted surface, roll out the pastry dough thinly and cut out 12 circles using the cutter. Press one circle into each of the holes of the muffin pan. Prick the base of each pie and chill in the refrigerator for a further 30 minutes.

Preheat the oven to 200°C (400°F) Gas 6.

Line the pastry cases with baking parchment, fill with baking beans and bake blind for about 10–15 minutes in the centre of the oven, until the pastry is golden brown. Let cool and remove the baking beans and parchment, then brush the insides of the pastry cases with a thin layer of melted chocolate. Let set.

To prepare the crème pâtissière, whisk together the cornflour, rosewater, sugar, egg and egg yolk until creamy. Put the milk and cream in a saucepan and bring to the boil. Pour over the egg mixture immediately, whisking all the time. Return to the pan and cook for a few minutes, until thick. Pass through a sieve/strainer to remove any lumps and let cool.

To assemble, spoon the rose crème pâtissière into a piping bag fitted with a large round nozzle and pipe into the cases. Top with the raspberries and chopped pistachios.

To glaze, heat the apricot glaze in a saucepan until just melted, cool slightly and then brush over the raspberries using a pastry brush.

Cherry & almond bakewell tarts

3 tablespoons good-quality cherry jam/jelly

1 quantity of Frangipane (see page 156)

50 g/⅔ cup flaked/slivered almonds

3–4 glacé cherries (or top with a fresh cherry for an extra summer hit)

ALMOND PASTRY

175 g/1⅓ cups plain/all-purpose flour, plus extra for dusting

25 g/¼ cup ground almonds

a pinch of salt

100 g/7 tablespoons butter, chilled and diced

25 g/2½ tablespoons icing/confectioners' sugar

1 egg, lightly beaten

FROSTING

100 g/⅔ cup icing/confectioners' sugar

½ teaspoon almond extract

10-cm/4-in. round cookie cutter

12 x 7-cm/3-in. fluted tart pans or a 12-hole muffin pan, greased

MAKES 12

These dainty tarts have a crisp almond pastry, cherry and amaretto jam/jelly, soft buttery frangipane, topped with almond flavoured icing, with crystallized almonds and a little slither of cherry.

Start by making the almond pastry. Tip the flour and ground almonds into the bowl of a food processor, add the salt and the butter. Using the pulse button rub the butter into the flour until it is pale sand-like in texture. Add the icing sugar and pulse again to combine. Add the beaten egg and pulse again until the dough starts to come together.

Tip out onto the work surface and use your hands to bring it together into a neat ball. Flatten into a disc, cover in clingfilm/plastic wrap and chill for at least 1 hour until firm.

Roll out the chilled pastry on a lightly floured work surface to a thickness of no more than 2 mm/¹⁄₁₆ in. Stamp out as many discs as you can using the cookie cutter. Gather the scraps together, re-roll and stamp out more discs. Gently press the pastry discs into the tart pans, trying not to stretch the dough but making sure that the pans are evenly lined.

Arrange the pans on a baking sheet and chill for 20 minutes while you preheat the oven to 170°C (350°F) Gas 3. Place another solid baking sheet on the middle shelf of the oven to heat up while it preheats.

Spread ½ teaspoon of jam into each tart shell and divide the frangipane evenly between the tarts – spreading it to evenly cover the jam.

Carefully transfer the individual pans to the hot baking sheet from the oven and bake in the preheated oven for about 20 minutes until the frangipane and pastry are golden and the pastry is crisp.

While the oven is hot, lightly toast the almonds on a baking sheet for 4 minutes until golden. Leave the tarts to cool in the pans for 30 minutes, then transfer to a wire rack to cool completely.

To make the frosting, sift the icing sugar into a bowl, add a drop or two of almond extract and enough water to make a smooth liquid that will coat the back of a spoon. Neatly spoon the icing over the frangipane in each tart and press the toasted almond bits around the edge. Top each tart with a slither of glacé cherry and leave to set before serving.

Pineapple & passion fruit curd tartlets

double quantity of Pâte
    Sucrée (see page 150)
plain/all-purpose flour,
    for dusting
1 small fresh pineapple,
    peeled, cored and sliced
4 passion fruit

PASSION FRUIT CURD
6 ripe, juicy passion fruit
freshly squeezed juice of
    1 small lemon, strained
75 g/¾ sick butter, cubed
3 large/US extra-large
    eggs, beaten
225 g/generous 1 cup
    caster/superfine sugar

7.5-cm/3-in. fluted cookie
    cutter
12-hole muffin pan, greased

MAKES 12

These tiny tartlets are like a bite of summer on a plate and will
burst with summery flavours with every mouthful.

First, prepare the passion fruit curd. Cut the 6 passion fruit in half,
scoop out the flesh and press through a sieve/strainer into a medium
bowl to extract the juice. Add the lemon juice, butter, eggs and sugar
and set over a saucepan of simmering water (or cook in a double boiler).

Cook, stirring all the time, for about 20 minutes or until the curd has
thickened considerably. If you are brave enough, you can cook this
over direct heat, watching that it doesn't get too hot and curdle. Strain
into a bowl and set aside.

Preheat the oven to 180°C (350°F) Gas 4.

Roll out the pastry thinly on a lightly floured work surface and cut
out 12 rounds with the cutter. Line the muffin pan with the pastry,
pressing it into the holes. Prick the bases and chill or freeze for
15 minutes. Bake blind for 5–6 minutes without lining with beans.
Let cool.

When ready to serve, fill the tartlet cases with a spoonful of passion
fruit curd, then top with sliced pineapple. Cut the 4 passion fruit in half,
scoop out the flesh and spoon a little, seeds and all, over each tartlet.
Serve immediately before the tartlets have a chance to go soggy.

Mango & passion fruit mini eclairs

1 quantity of Crème Diplomate (see page 155, made with mango and passion fruit Crème Pâtissière)

PÂTE À CHOUX
125 ml/½ cup milk
100 g/7 tablespoons butter
a pinch of salt
a pinch of sugar
140 g/1 cup plain/ all-purpose flour
approximately 6 eggs

CRUMBLE TOPPING
80 g/¾ sick butter, softened
100 g/½ cup light brown sugar
100 g/¾ cup plain/ all-purpose flour

baking sheets, lined with baking parchment
piping/pastry bag fitted with a plain nozzle/tip

MAKES ABOUT 20

Filled with a punchy tropical pastry cream and topped with a crunchy crumble, these beauties will definitely have your guests asking for more at any summer event!

First, make the crumble topping. Beat the butter and sugar together in a stand mixer or in a bowl with an electric whisk just until well combined. Add the flour and bring together into a dough with your hands. Turn the dough out onto a sheet of baking parchment, top with another sheet and flatten with a rolling pin until about 3 mm/⅛ in. thick. Freeze for 1 hour.

Preheat the oven to 180°C (350°F) Gas 4.

Put the milk, butter, salt and sugar in a medium saucepan over medium heat and add 125 ml/½ cup water. Stir constantly so that the sugar doesn't burn and cause the mixture to stick to the bottom of the pan. When it comes to the boil, quickly stir in the flour and mix together. Beat the dough vigorously until it cleanly leaves the sides of the saucepan – this can take up to 5 minutes, depending on the heat.

Transfer the dough to a stand mixer or mixing bowl (using an electric whisk) and beat in the eggs, one at a time. You might not need all 6 eggs – flour and eggs behave differently no matter how many times you make the same recipe, so the number of eggs needed can vary. When it is soft and smooth and drops off a spoon leaving behind a 'V' shape, it is ready.

Spoon the dough into the piping bag. Pipe ovals onto the baking sheet, 5 cm/2 in. long and spaced apart. Bake in the preheated oven for 10–15 minutes until golden brown and hollow in the middle.

Take the crumble topping out of the freezer, remove the top sheet of paper and cut into long, slim rectangles to fit on the éclairs. Place a rectangle on top of each éclair. Bake for 10–12 minutes or until puffed up and golden, then turn the oven off and leave the éclairs inside to cool completely and dry out.

Carefully cut each cooled éclair in half horizontally. Fill the piping bag with Crème Diplomate and pipe a generous coil along the cut side of the bottom half of each éclair. Sandwich with the other half of the éclair. If you like, in order to boost the mango flavour in this recipe, you could put some mango flesh and icing/confectioners' sugar in a blender and process until smooth. Spoon some of this on the bottom half of each éclair, then pipe the Crème Diplomate over it.

Mini strawberry tarts

100 g/7 tablespoons
  butter, softened
50 g/⅓ cup icing/
  confectioners' sugar
a pinch of salt
1 egg, lightly beaten
1 teaspoon vanilla bean
  paste
175 g/1⅓ cups plain/
  all-purpose flour, plus
  extra for dusting
1 quantity of Crème
  Pâtissière (see page 154,
  either made plain or
  boozy)

TO DECORATE
400 g/4 cups strawberries,
  hulled
4 tablespoons apricot
  jam/jelly
edible gold leaf (optional)

8–9-cm/3¼–3½-in.
  round cookie cutter
12 x 7-cm/3-in. mini
  tart pans or a 12-hole
  muffin pan, greased
baking beans (optional)

MAKES 12

Afternoon tea just isn't complete without a strawberry tart! Classically filled with a vanilla crème pâtissière, here it can be made with a boozy version if liked to make the tart even more decadent.

Start by making the pastry. Cream the butter, sugar and salt together in a stand mixer or in a bowl with a handheld electric whisk until pale – this will take 3–4 minutes.

With the mixer running, gradually add the egg with the vanilla bean paste, mixing until fully incorporated. Gently mix in the flour but do not overwork the dough. Bring the dough together into a ball, wrap in clingfilm/plastic wrap, flatten into a disc and chill for at least 2 hours or until needed.

Roll out the pastry on a lightly floured work surface to a thickness of no more than 2 mm/1/16 in. Stamp out discs from the dough using the cookie cutter. Neatly line the tart pans with the pastry discs and trim off any excess with a small sharp knife. Prick the bases with a fork, line with a square of baking parchment or foil and fill with baking beans or rice. Arrange the pans on a baking sheet and chill in the refrigerator for 20 minutes.

Preheat the oven to 180°C (350°F) Gas 4.

Bake the pastry cases on the middle shelf of the preheated oven for about 10–12 minutes or until pale golden. Remove the baking beans or rice and parchment or foil and continue to cook for 1 minute until the bases are crisp. Remove from the oven and cool. Remove the cases and arrange on a tray.

Divide the crème pâtissière between the pastry cases and spread level. Leave to cool for 10 minutes.

Quarter the strawberries and arrange on top of the crème pâtissière. Warm the apricot jam – either in a small pan over low heat or in the microwave in short bursts. Pass through a fine mesh sieve/strainer to remove any lumps and gently brush over the top of the strawberries. Decorate each tart with a piece of gold leaf if you wish and leave for 30 minutes or so to allow the jam/jelly to set before serving.

Summer berry tartlets

110 g/¾ cup plain/
all-purpose flour,
plus extra for dusting

60 g/½ stick butter,
chilled and diced

30 g/2 tablespoons
caster/superfine sugar

1 egg yolk

a few drops of pure vanilla
extract

CRÈME PÂTISSIÈRE

1 tablespoon cornflour/
cornstarch

60 g/⅓ cup caster/
granulated sugar

1 egg and 1 egg yolk

100 ml/scant ½ cup milk

150 ml/⅔ cup double/
heavy cream

1 vanilla pod/bean, split
lengthways

TO ASSEMBLE

200 g/1½ cups summer
berries

3 tablespoons apricot jam/
jelly

freshly squeezed juice
of 2 small lemons

6-cm/2½-in. fluted cookie
cutter

24 mini tartlet pans,
greased

baking beans

piping/pastry bag fitted
with a round nozzle/tip

MAKES 24

These crisp pastry tartlets, filled with classic crème pâtissière and topped with glazed summer berries, are guaranteed to disappear very quickly whenever you serve them!

To make the pastry, sift the flour into a mixing bowl and rub in the butter until the mixture resembles fine breadcrumbs. Add the sugar, egg yolk and vanilla extract and mix together to a soft dough with your fingers, adding a little cold water if the mixture is too dry. Wrap in clingfilm/plastic wrap and chill in the refrigerator for 1 hour.

Preheat the oven to 180°C (350°F) Gas 4.

On a flour-dusted surface, roll out the pastry to a thickness of 3 mm/ ⅛ in. Stamp out 24 rounds using the cutter and press one into each mini tartlet pan, trimming away any excess pastry. Chill in the refrigerator for 30 minutes. Line each pastry case with baking parchment and fill with baking beans. Bake in the preheated oven for 12–15 minutes, until golden brown and crisp. Leave to cool in the pans for 10 minutes, then transfer to a wire rack and leave to cool completely.

To prepare the crème pâtissière, whisk together the cornflour/cornstarch, sugar, egg and egg yolk until creamy. Put the milk, cream and split vanilla pod/bean in a saucepan and bring to the boil. Pour over the egg mixture, whisking all the time. Return to the pan and cook for a few minutes until thick, then remove the vanilla pod/bean. Pass the mixture through a sieve/strainer to remove any lumps and set aside to cool.

To assemble, spoon the crème pâtissière into the piping bag and pipe it into the pastry cases. Top each one with berries. Put the apricot jam and lemon juice in a small saucepan and heat until blended. Pass through a sieve/strainer to remove any bits and, using a pastry brush, brush the mixture over each tartlet to glaze.

These tartlets are best eaten on the day they are made.

Lemon profiteroles

LEMON PASTRY CREAM

375 ml/1½ cups full-fat/
  whole milk

½ vanilla pod/bean, split
  lengthways

3 large/US extra-large egg
  yolks

125 g/⅔ cup caster/
  granulated sugar

45 g/5 tablespoons Italian
  '00' plain/all-purpose
  flour

finely grated zest of
  2 lemons

PROFITEROLES

125 g/ 1 stick plus 1
  tablespoon butter, diced,
  plus extra for greasing

1 teaspoon caster/
  granulated sugar

a pinch of salt

125 g/scant 1 cup Italian
  '00' plain/all-purpose
  flour

4 large/US extra-large eggs

TO SERVE

250 ml/1 cup double/
  heavy cream

zest of 1 lemon,
  cut into thin strips

2 large baking sheets,
  buttered

piping/pastry bag, fitted
  with a 1-cm/½-in. plain
  nozzle/tip

piping/pastry bag, fitted
  with a 5-mm/¼-in. plain
  nozzle/tip

SERVES 8

Fresh and zingy lemons are a quintessential summer flavour and lend themselves triumphantly to these bite-sized choux buns.

To make the lemon pastry cream, place the milk and the vanilla pod/bean in a medium saucepan. Heat over medium-low heat until scalded (just up to boiling point). While the milk is heating, whisk together the egg yolks and sugar in a large bowl. Add the flour and stir until completely dissolved. Slowly whisk one-third of the scalded milk into the egg yolk mixture. Add the remaining milk all at once and blend thoroughly.

Pour the mixture back into the pan and return it to the heat. Stir until the cream has thickened. Turn off the heat, add the zest and continue to stir for 1 minute. Remove the vanilla pod/bean. Pour the mixture into a bowl and place a piece of baking parchment on top to stop a skin forming.

Preheat the oven to 220°C (425°F) Gas 7.

To make the profiteroles, combine 250 ml/1 cup cold water with the butter, sugar and salt in a medium-heavy saucepan over medium-low heat. As soon as it reaches the boil, remove the pan from the heat.

Add all the flour at once and stir with a wooden spoon. When the flour is thoroughly blended, return the pan to the heat. Stir vigorously for 1–2 minutes, or until the mixture pulls away from the sides of the pan, forming a ball of dough. Remove the pan from the heat and rest it on a damp kitchen cloth. Beat in the eggs, one at a time, incorporating each egg thoroughly before adding the next.

Spoon the mixture into the piping bag fitted with the larger nozzle/tip. Pipe 24 small mounds of dough 4 cm/1½ in. in diameter and spaced about 5 cm/2 in. apart on the baking sheets. Moisten your index finger with water and gently flatten the pointed peaks. Place the baking sheets in the oven, staggered so that they are not on top of each other. Bake for 20 minutes, or until golden. Rotate the baking sheets after 15 minutes so the profiteroles bake evenly. Turn off the oven and cool the profiteroles in the oven with the door ajar.

To serve, beat half the cream until stiff. Stir this cream into the lemon pastry cream, then spoon this mixture into the piping bag fitted with the smaller nozzle. Make a small slit in the side of each profiterole and fill with the pastry cream. Stack the profiteroles on a serving plate, sprinkle with lemon zest and serve immediately with the rest of the cream.

Strawberry & pistachio tartlets

1 quantity of Pâte Sablée (see page 150)

plain/all-purpose flour, for dusting

1 quantity of Crème Pâtissière (see page 154)

50 g/¼ cup pistachio paste (storebought)

25 g/1 oz. white chocolate

250 g/9 oz. strawberries, hulled and halved or quartered

50 g/⅓ cup pistachios, finely chopped

6 individual tartlet pans, greased and lightly dusted with flour

baking beans

MAKES 6

The pistachio paste produces an amazing vibrant green colour and flavour that works so well with juicy summer strawberries. Pistachio paste can be bought online, or to make your own, see below.

Preheat the oven to 180°C (350°F) Gas 4.

Take the pâte sablée out of the refrigerator and divide it into 6 equal portions. Using a rolling pin, roll out each portion on a lightly floured surface to a rough circle slightly larger than the tartlet pans.

Loosely wrap one portion of dough at a time around the rolling pin and transfer it to a prepared tartlet pan. Unravel the dough into the pan. Gently coax the dough neatly into the curves and angles of the pan, press lightly into the sides and cut off any excess with a small, sharp knife.

Lay a piece of baking parchment over each pan and fill it with baking beans. Put all the pans on a baking sheet and bake in the preheated oven for about 10–15 minutes.

Lower the oven temperature to 160°C (325°F) Gas 3. Remove the paper and beans from the tartlet pans and return the tartlet cases to the oven for 5 minutes. Remove the tartlet cases from the oven and allow to cool completely, then remove from the pans.

Meanwhile, melt the chocolate on low power in a microwave or in a heatproof bowl over a pan of simmering water (not letting the base of the bowl touch the water). Brush the melted chocolate inside the cooled tartlet cases.

Stir the pistachio paste through the crème pâtissière in a mixing bowl. Divide the pistachio crème pâtissière evenly between the tartlet cases. Top the tartlets with the strawberries and chopped pistachios.

Note: To make your own pistachio paste, put 100 g/⅔ cup pistachios and 50 g/¼ cup caster/superfine sugar into a heavy-based saucepan and continually stir over medium heat until the sugar crystallizes around the nuts and they turn golden. Remove from the heat and scatter onto a sheet of baking parchment. Allow to cool completely. Break the cooled nuts into pieces and put in a food processor. Process to a powder, then add 1 tablespoon vegetable oil and process again until you get a paste. Store, refrigerated, in an airtight container for up to 2 weeks.

Summer fruit jam tarts

150 g/1 stick plus 2
  tablespoons butter,
  softened
100 g/½ cup caster/
  granulated sugar
3 egg yolks
200 g/1½ cups plain/
  all-purpose flour
½ teaspoon baking powder
a pinch of salt
grated zest of 1 lemon
grated zest of 1 orange
8 tablespoons good-quality
  jams/jellies and curds of
  your choosing

7-cm/3-in. fluted cookie
  cutter
2 x 12-hole muffin pans,
  greased

MAKES 24

Fill these childhood favourites with the wonderful flavours of summer jams - even better if you can use homemade jams made from the freshest summer fruits.

Combine the butter with the sugar in the bowl of a stand mixer and beat until pale and light – this will take about 5 minutes.

Gradually add the egg yolks one at a time and mix until they are thoroughly combined. Sift the flour and baking powder into the bowl. Add the salt and grated citrus zest and fold in using a rubber spatula or large metal spoon. The dough will be soft and buttery.

Gather the dough together, form a ball and flatten into a disc. Cover with clingfilm/plastic wrap and chill in the refrigerator for at least 2 hours until firm.

Preheat the oven to 180°C (350°F) Gas 4.

Roll out the dough on a lightly floured work surface to a thickness of 2 mm/1⁄16 in.

Using the cutter, stamp out discs from the dough and gently press into the prepared muffin pans.

Drop a teaspoonful of jam or curd into each tart and bake on the middle shelf of the preheated oven for about 12 minutes until the pastry is golden brown and the jam is bubbling.

Leave to cool for a few minutes before transferring to a wire rack to cool completely – the jam and curd needs to set before serving.

Individual plum tartes tatin

100 g/½ cup caster/
  superfine sugar
50 g/3½ tablespoons
  butter
6 ripe plums
60 g/2 oz. golden
  marzipan
plain/all-purpose flour,
  for dusting
375 g/13 oz. storebought
  all-butter puff pastry
  (thawed if frozen)
custard or whipped cream,
  to serve

12-hole muffin pan, greased
9-cm/3½-in round cookie
  cutter

MAKES 12

Caramelized tartes tatin, with their rich buttery pastry and dark sugary caramel, are quite simply delicious. Whilst normally served as a large tart, these individual ones make the perfect sweet treat. You can substitute other fruits, such as apple, pear or pineapple, if you prefer.

Preheat the oven to 180°C (350°F) Gas 4.

Put the sugar and butter in a small saucepan and warm over gentle heat, until the sugar dissolves and then allow it to caramelize and turn golden brown, taking care that it does not burn. Remove from the heat immediately and put a spoonful of caramel into each hole of the pan.

Cut the plums in half, and remove the stones/pits. Place one plum half, cut-side up, in each hole of the pan.

Break the marzipan into 12 pieces of equal size and roll them into balls. Place one ball into each plum, where the stone/pit once was.

On a flour-dusted surface, roll the pastry out to a thickness of 3 mm/ ⅛ in. Stamp out 12 rounds with the cutter. Cover each plum with a pastry round, pressing the pastry tightly into the holes.

Bake the tarts in the preheated oven for 12–15 minutes, until the pastry is crisp and the plums are soft. Remove from the oven, leave to cool for a few minutes, then remove each tatin with a spoon and invert.

Serve the tatins warm or cold with cream or custard.

Raspberry & rose millefeuilles

The millefeuille is a French institution. Meaning 'a thousand leaves', it consists of layers of crisp puff pastry. This recipe is a little twist on the French classic, perfect for a summer's day, with fresh raspberries, delicate rose flavours and served with a glass of rosé Champagne.

250 g/9 oz. storebought all-butter puff pastry (thawed if frozen)

plain/all-purpose flour, for dusting

½ quantity Crème Diplomate (see page 155)

1 teaspoon rosewater

1 punnet raspberries

icing/confectioners' sugar, for dusting

6-cm/2½-in. round cookie cutter

baking sheet, lined with baking parchment

piping/pastry bag fitted with a plain nozzle/tip

kitchen blowtorch

MAKES 8

Preheat the oven to 180°C (350°F) Gas 4.

Using a rolling pin, roll out the pastry on a lightly floured surface until 5 mm/¼ in. thick.

Stamp out about 8 rounds using the cookie cutter and arrange them on the prepared baking sheet.

Bake the rounds of pastry in the preheated oven for about 10 minutes or until puffed up and golden. Allow to cool completely.

Make the crème diplomate following the instructions on page 155, then fold in the rosewater at the end.

Using a serrated knife, cut through each pastry round twice, horizontally, to make 3 layers.

Fill the piping bag with crème diplomate and pipe 4 bulbs of cream around the rim of the flat layers of pastry (leave the domed layers for the tops of the millefeuilles). Leave space to fit a raspberry after each bulb.

Pipe a bulb in the centre of each pastry round.

Fill the gaps between the bulbs of cream with upside-down raspberries.

Lay all the pastry tops, domed side up, on a heatproof surface and dust them liberally with icing/confectioners' sugar. Briefly blast them with a kitchen blowtorch to caramelize them and give them extra crunch.

Assemble the millefeuilles, putting the caramelized domes on the tops.

Chocolate & cherry tarts

HAZELNUT PASTRY

150 g/1 cup plus
   2 tablespoons plain/
   all-purpose flour, plus
   extra for dusting
50 g/½ cup ground
   hazelnuts
½ teaspoon ground
   cinnamon
a pinch of salt
100 g/7 tablespoons
   butter, chilled and diced
25 g/1½ tablespoons
   icing/confectioners' sugar
1 egg, lightly beaten

HAZELNUT GANACHE

75 ml/scant ⅓ cup
   whipping cream
100 g/¾ cup chopped
   dark/bittersweet
   chocolate
75 g/generous ½ cup
   chopped milk/semisweet
   chocolate
20 g/1 tablespoon honey
50 g/3½ tablespoons
   hazelnut purée/butter

TO DECORATE

cherry jam/jelly
200 g/1½ cup chopped
   dark/bittersweet
   chocolate
red lustre powder
   (optional)
12 fresh cherries

10-cm/4-in. round cookie
   cutter
12-hole muffin pan, greased
baking beans
disposable piping/pastry
   bag

MAKES 12

Fresh and juicy cherries at the height of summer pack a whole punch of sunny flavours into these delicate little tarts.

Start by making the hazelnut pastry. Tip the flour and ground hazelnuts into the bowl of a food processor, add the cinnamon, salt and butter. Pulse to rub the butter into the flour until it is pale and sand-like in texture. Add the icing/confectioners' sugar and mix again to combine. Add the beaten egg and pulse until the mixture starts to come together. Tip the dough out onto the work surface and use your hands to bring it together to a neat ball. Flatten into a disc, cover in clingfilm/plastic wrap and chill in the refrigerator for at least 1 hour until firm.

Roll the dough out on a lightly floured work surface to a thickness of no more than 2 mm/¹⁄₁₆ in. Using the cookie cutter stamp out 12 discs from the dough. Gently press the discs into the muffin pan, trying not to stretch the dough but making sure that the holes are evenly lined. Chill in the refrigerator for 20 minutes.

Preheat the oven to 170°C (350°F) Gas 5.

Line the tart cases with a square of baking parchment and fill with baking beans. Bake in the preheated oven for 10 minutes until pale golden and starting to crisp. Remove the tarts from the oven and carefully lift out the baking beans or rice and parchment or foil, and return the pan to the oven for 1 minute more to dry out the tart bases. Remove from the oven and leave until cold before removing from the pan.

Temper the chocolate for decorating by melting in the microwave in bursts of 30 seconds. Once the mixture is three-quarters melted, stop heating and stir well to remove any lumps. Spread out very thinly onto a sheet of baking parchment using a palette knife and set aside to harden. Once set, brush with red lustre powder.

Next, prepare the ganache. Tip all of the ganache ingredients into a heatproof bowl and set over a pan of barely simmering water. Stir gently to combine into a silky smooth mixture, remove from the heat and leave to cool for 15 minutes. Transfer to the piping bag and set aside.

To build the tarts, divide the cherry compote between the pastry cases and spread level. Pipe ganache over the cherry compote in an even, smooth layer. Finish each tart with a fresh cherry and crack the tempered chocolate to form shards that can be arranged on top.

Caramelized tartes au citron

110 g/¾ cup plain/all-purpose flour, plus extra for dusting

60 g/½ stick butter, chilled and diced

finely grated zest of 2 lemons

2 tablespoons caster/superfine sugar

1 egg yolk

icing/confectioners' sugar, for dusting

LEMON FILLING

100 ml/⅓ cup double/heavy cream

finely grated zest and juice of 1 lemon

50 g/¼ cup caster/superfine sugar

1 egg

20 oval mini tartlet pans (8 cm/3¼ in. long), greased

baking beans

kitchen blowtorch (optional)

MAKES 20

These melt-in-the-mouth tartlets are mini versions of a classic French lemon tart – a delicious combination of buttery pastry, tangy lemon cream filling and a caramelized sugar topping.

To make the pastry, sift the flour into a mixing bowl and rub in the butter until the mixture resembles fine breadcrumbs. Add the lemon zest, sugar and egg yolk and mix together to a soft dough with your fingertips, adding a little cold water if the mixture is too dry. Wrap the dough in clingfilm/plastic wrap and chill in the refrigerator for 1 hour.

Preheat the oven to 180°C (350°F) Gas 4.

On a flour-dusted surface, roll out the pastry to a thickness of 3 mm/⅛ in. Use a sharp knife to cut out 20 oval pieces of pastry and press one into each tartlet pan, trimming the edges with a sharp knife. Put a piece of baking parchment in each pastry case, fill with baking beans and bake in the preheated oven for 10–15 minutes, until the pastry is crisp. Do not turn off the oven.

To make the lemon filling, whisk together the cream, lemon juice and zest, sugar and egg and pour into each pastry case. Bake the tartlets in the preheated oven for 10–15 minutes, until the filling has set.

Dust the tarts with sifted icing sugar, then caramelize the sugar using a blowtorch or under a hot grill/broiler. Leave to cool before serving.

Passion fruit meringue tarts

100 g/7 tablespoons butter, softened

50 g/⅓ cup icing/confectioners' sugar

a pinch of salt

1 egg, lightly beaten

1 teaspoon vanilla bean paste

175 g/1⅓ cups plain/all-purpose flour, plus extra for dusting

1 tablespoon freeze-dried passion fruit powder

350 g/¾ lb. storebought passion fruit curd, for the filling

1 quantity of Italian Meringue (see page 157)

9-cm/3½-in. round cookie cutter

12 x 7-cm/3-in. shallow mini tart pans

baking beans (optional)

sugar thermometer

disposable piping/pastry bag (optional)

kitchen blowtorch

MAKES 12

These really are a little tangy sensation! A crisp pastry flavoured with freeze-dried passion fruit powder filled with a passion fruit curd and topped with Italian meringue.

Cream the butter, icing sugar and salt together in a stand mixer or in a large mixing bowl with a handheld electric whisk until pale – this will take 3–4 minutes.

With the mixer running, gradually add the beaten egg with the vanilla bean paste, mixing until fully incorporated. Gently mix in the flour and passionfruit powder but do not overwork the dough. Bring the dough together into a ball, wrap in clingfilm/plastic wrap, flatten into a disc and chill in the refrigerator for at least 2 hours or until needed.

Roll out the dough on a lightly floured work surface to an even thickness of no more than 2 mm/¹⁄₁₆ in. Stamp out discs using the cookie cutter. Neatly line the tart pans with the discs and trim off any excess from the top with a small sharp knife. Prick the bases with a fork, line with a square of foil or baking parchment and fill with baking beans or rice. Arrange the pans on a baking sheet and chill in the refrigerator for 20 minutes.

Preheat the oven to 180°C (350°F) Gas 4.

Bake on the middle shelf of the oven for 10–12 minutes or until pale golden. Remove the beans or rice and foil and baking parchment and continue to cook for 1 minute until the bases are crisp. Remove from the oven and set aside to cool.

Divide the passion fruit curd between the baked tart shells and chill for 20 minutes while you prepare the meringue.

Prepare the Italian meringue following the instructions on page 157 and, working quickly, either spoon the prepared Italian meringue on top of the passion fruit tarts or fill a piping bag and pipe peaks on top.

Light the blowtorch and lightly scorch the meringue. Leave to cool before serving.

Blackcurrant millefeuilles

375 g/13 oz. storebought all-butter puff pastry (thawed if frozen)

1 egg, beaten

caster/superfine sugar, for sprinkling

icing/confectioners' sugar, for dusting

FILLING

200 ml/¾ cup double/ heavy cream

2 generous tablespoons blackcurrant preserve

baking sheet, greased and lined with baking parchment

piping/pastry bag fitted with a small star nozzle/ tip

MAKES 24

In a twist on the traditional filling of vanilla custard, these pastries contain blackcurrant preserve made from fresh summery currants – it provides a sharp fruity burst, perfectly offsetting the cream and sugar dusting to create these delicate little pastries.

Preheat the oven to 180°C (350°F) Gas 4.

On a flour-dusted surface, roll out the pastry to a rectangle about 3 mm/⅛ in. thick. Cut into 6 strips of 30 x 4 cm/12 x 1½ in. and transfer to the prepared baking sheet using a large spatula, leaving a gap between each strip of pastry. Brush with the beaten egg and sprinkle over a little caster sugar.

Bake the pastry in the preheated oven for 12–15 minutes, until risen and golden brown on top. Transfer to a wire rack and leave to cool completely. When you are ready to assemble the millefeuilles, cut each pastry strip into 8 small squares.

Whip the cream to stiff peaks and spoon into the piping bag. Pipe a row of small cream stars onto half of the pastry squares, top with a small spoonful of blackcurrant preserve, then cover with a second pastry square. Repeat until all the pastry squares are filled, then dust the tops of each pastry with icing sugar.

Serve immediately or store in the refrigerator until needed.

SHORTCRUST PASTRY

150 g/1 cup plus 2 tablespoons plain/all-purpose flour, plus extra for dusting
150 g/1 stick plus 2 tablespoons butter, chilled and cubed
75 g/⅓ cup caster/superfine sugar
75 g/½ cup plus 1 tablespoon rice flour
grated zest of ½ lemon

FILLING

1 vanilla pod/bean
2 egg yolks
200 g/scant 1 cup clotted cream
80 g/⅓ cup caster/superfine sugar
a pinch of flaky sea salt
250 g/2 cups fresh raspberries
3 tablespoons icing/confectioners' sugar

6 tartlet pans with removable base, about 10 cm/4 in. diameter
kitchen blowtorch

MAKES 6

Clotted cream & raspberry brûlée tartlets

These flavours are the perfect combination for sunny summer afternoons – the flavours of an afternoon tea of scones and jam in a dainty little tartlet.

Preheat the oven to 180°C (350°F) Gas 4.

Rub together the flour, butter, sugar and rice flour until the mixture looks like breadcrumbs. Stir in the lemon zest and bring it together to form a dough. Chill until firm, then roll out on a lightly floured surface and line the pans, then return them to the refrigerator to chill.

Split the vanilla pods lengthwise and scrape out the seeds. Beat the egg yolks, clotted cream, sugar, vanilla seeds and salt until smooth.

Bake the shortcrust bases for 6–8 minutes, until firm and pale golden. If the shortcrust has risen up slightly, simply push it back carefully against the edges with a teaspoon. Remove from the oven and scatter the raspberries over the bases. Pour in the custard filling. Bake in the preheated oven for 10–15 minutes. Remove from the oven and leave to cool.

Sprinkle a fine layer of icing sugar over the top of each tart and caramelize carefully with a blowtorch, taking care not to burn any raspberries that may be peeping out of the custard. Serve within a couple of hours, so that the brûlée top remains lovely and crisp.

Lemon & lime meringue tartlets

PASTRY
200 g/1½ cups plain/ all-purpose flour
100 g/7 tablespoons butter, softened
20 g/scant ¼ cup ground almonds
60 g/7 tablespoons icing/ confectioners' sugar, plus extra for dusting
1 egg yolk

TARTLET FILLING
2 eggs
1 egg yolk
30 g/2½ tablespoons caster/superfine sugar
150 ml/⅔ cup double/ heavy cream
grated zest and freshly squeezed juice of 1 lemon
grated zest and freshly squeezed juice of 1 lime

MERINGUE
2 egg whites
½ teaspoon pure vanilla extract
75 g/6 tablespoons caster/superfine sugar

6 small fluted tartlet pans or rings
sugar thermometer
kitchen blowtorch

MAKES 6

Surprisingly simple to make, with a little practice, these tartlets combine the tangy flavours of both lemons and limes for an extra citrus summer punch.

Preheat the oven to 160°C (325°F) Gas 3.

For the pastry, blitz the flour, butter and almonds together in a food processor before adding the icing/confectioners' sugar, then the egg yolk. Continue to blitz until it forms a ball. Roll out the pastry to a thickness of about 2 cm/¾ in. Wrap it in some clingfilm/plastic wrap and place in the refrigerator for an hour to chill.

Once the pastry is chilled, divide into 6 and roll each of these out to a thickness of about 3 mm/⅛ in. (dust the pastry with a little icing sugar to stop it sticking). Place the pastry into the small tartlet pans or rings, covering the base and sides. Place the tartlet bases in the refrigerator for a further 30 minutes to relax the gluten in the flour.

Prick the tartlet bases with a fork to stop them rising and bake in the oven for 10 minutes until just cooked but still pale.

For the tartlet filling, whisk the eggs, egg yolk, sugar, cream, and juice and zest of the lemon and lime together, before carefully pouring into the tartlet bases. Bake for 7–9 minutes, checking after 7 minutes to see whether the mix has just set, it should still wobble a little when shaken.

To make the meringue, you will need a spotlessly clean mixing bowl (wipe it with a little vinegar, or lemon juice, to remove any oil which will stop the meringue from setting firm).

Whisk the egg whites and vanilla to soft peaks.

Next, make a sugar syrup. In a heavy-bottomed saucepan, add enough water to just cover the base, then add the sugar and heat until the mixture is boiling and the temperature reaches 115°C/240°F.

Now, while continuing to whisk the egg whites, pour the hot sugar syrup in a slow stream into the mixing bowl. Keep whisking until firm peaks are formed. Spoon or pipe the Italian meringue onto the tartlets and use a blowtorch to caramelize it. Serve as they are, or gently warmed for 10 minutes in a very low oven to make them extra special.

Raspberry squares

200 g/⅔ cup good-quality
  raspberry jam/jelly
300 g/2½ cups icing/
  confectioners' sugar
1–3 tablespoons hot water
sprinkles, to decorate

SWEET SHORTCRUST
PASTRY DOUGH
200 g/1¾ sticks butter,
  chilled and diced
350 g/2⅔ cups
  plain/all-purpose flour
125 g/1 cup plus
  1 tablespoon icing/
  confectioners' sugar
1 teaspoon pure vanilla
  extract OR seeds from
  ½ vanilla pod/bean
1 egg

*2 baking sheets, greased
and lined with baking
parchment*

MAKES 12–16

These delicious pastry squares packed full of juicy raspberry jam and topped with oozing icing and sprinkles make the prettiest adornment to any summer table.

First, make the pastry. Rub the cold butter into the flour until sandy in texture, then add the icing sugar and vanilla. Add the whole egg and mix until the dough holds together and becomes smooth, taking care not to over-mix. You can also make the dough in the food processor by pulsing the ingredients together briefly, if you wish. Wrap the dough in clingfilm/plastic wrap and chill for at least 30 minutes in the refrigerator before using.

Preheat the oven to 180°C (350°F) Gas 4.

Split the sweet shortcrust pastry dough into 2 equal portions and roll into 2 evenly sized squares, around 3 mm/⅛ in. thick. Each one should be around 30 x 30 cm/12 x 12 in. Ensure the shapes are the same size as you will be layering them later.

Put the pastry squares on the prepared baking sheets. Prick the surfaces with a fork to prevent air bubbles forming as they bake. Pop in the preheated oven to bake for about 10–12 minutes or until slightly golden. Remove from the oven and set aside to cool on a wire rack.

On one of the cooled pastry sheets, spread a generous, even layer of the raspberry jam/jelly. Very carefully, slide the other piece of pastry on top so that it sits exactly on top of the base. Handle delicately, as the pastry can break quite easily.

Mix the icing sugar with hot water to form a smooth paste. The amount of water you will need varies depending on your sugar. If the paste is too thick, add a few drops more water. Too thin, add a bit more icing sugar. Aim for the consistency of runny honey. Spread the icing on top of the pastry to evenly cover. Top with sprinkles and leave to dry.

Using a very sharp knife, cut the edges off the pastry to make straight sides. Cut into 12 large or 16 small equal pieces to serve.

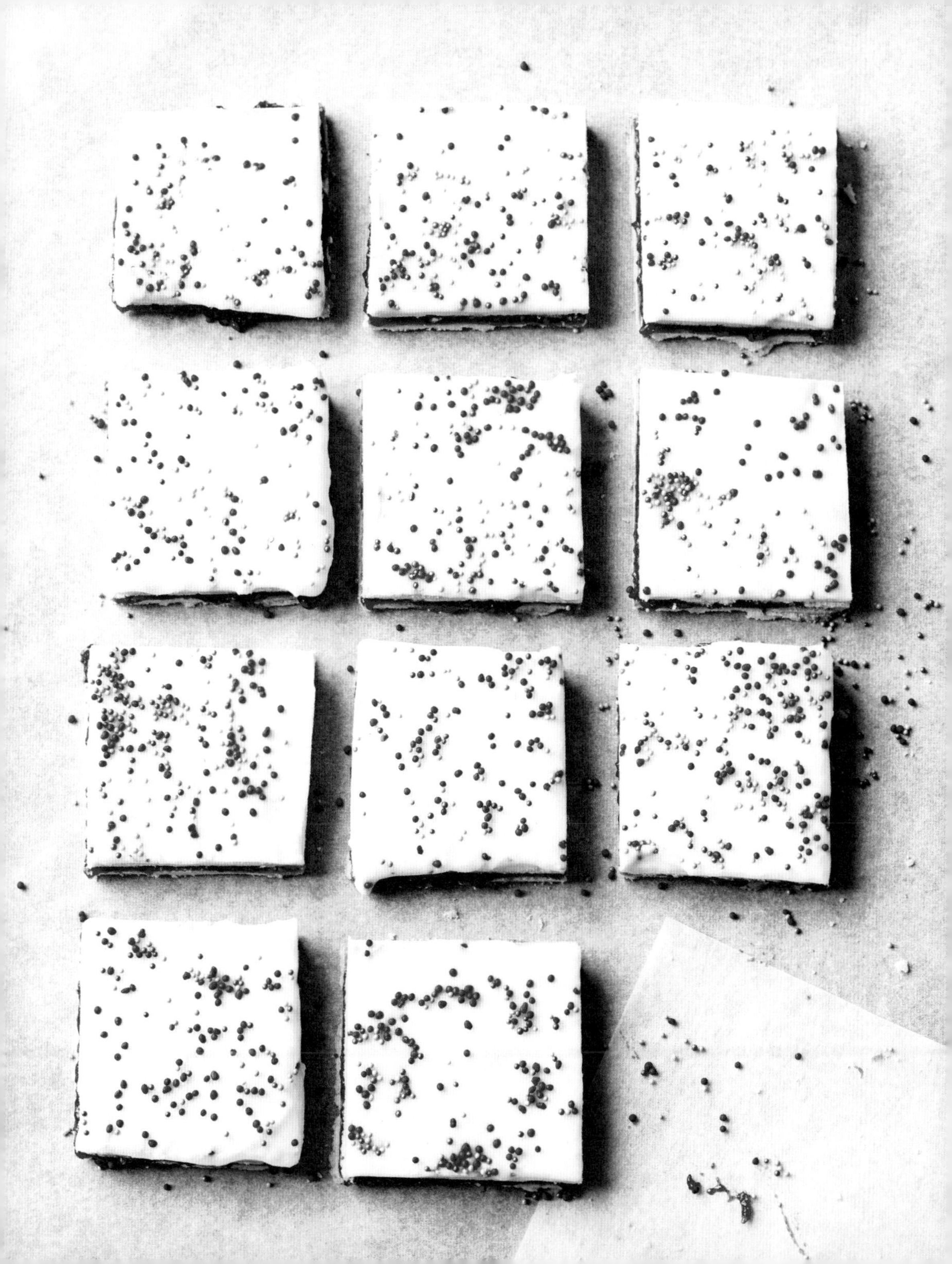

Lemon curd tartlets with rhubarb & ginger

350 g/12 oz. storebought shortcrust pastry (thawed if frozen)

plain/all-purpose flour, for dusting

1 quantity of Lemon Curd (see page 157)

edible flowers, to serve

RHUBARB & GINGER

675 g/6½ cups chopped fresh rhubarb

150 g/¾ cup caster/granulated sugar

170 g/½ cup honey

2 tablespoons finely chopped crystallized ginger

still-warm sterilized glass jars with airtight lids

10 x 7.5-cm/3-in. tartlet pans, greased and floured

baking beans

MAKES 10

The bright citrus lemon curd gives vibrancy to these bite-sized tartlets and enhances the delicious rhubarb and ginger making them the perfect summer sweet treat.

Preheat the oven to 180°C (350°F) Gas 4.

To make the rhubarb and ginger, trim the ends of the rhubarb and cut the stalks into 2.5-cm/1-in. pieces. In a non-reactive pan over medium–high heat, dissolve the sugar and honey in 475 ml/2 cups water. Add the rhubarb and ginger and bring to the boil. Reduce the heat and cook for a further 5 minutes. Pour the rhubarb into warm, sterilized glass jars and tap the jars on the counter top to get rid of air pockets. Wipe the jars clean and screw on the lids.

Fill a canning kettle with enough water to cover the height of the jars by 5 cm/2 in. and bring to the boil. Place the jars in the water bath. Cover with a lid and once the water has come back to the boil seal for 10 minutes. Remove the jars from the water bath and leave to cool.

Roll the pastry out onto a lightly floured surface into a large circle. Cut it into circles big enough to line the tart pans. Press the pastry circles into the pans, trim the edges and prick the bases with a fork. Cover with clingfilm/plastic wrap and chill for another 30 minutes.

Remove the tartlets from the refrigerator, line with baking parchment, and top with baking beans. Bake blind in the preheated oven for 5 minutes, then remove the paper and baking beans.

Return to the oven and bake for a further 8–10 minutes, until golden. Remove from the oven and cool on a wire rack.

To assemble, fill the tartlet shells with lemon curd, then top with a generous teaspoon of rhubarb and ginger. Sprinkle with edible flowers and serve.

Glazed strawberry tartlets

1 tablespoon cornflour/
   cornstarch
60 g/scant ⅓ cup caster/
   granulated sugar
1 egg plus 1 egg yolk
100 ml/scant ½ cup milk
150 ml/⅔ cup double/
   heavy cream
1 vanilla pod/bean,
   split lengthwise
300 g/1½ cups
   strawberries, hulled
   and halved
5 tablespoons apricot
   preserve
freshly squeezed juice
   of 2 small lemons

PASTRY
250 g/2 scant cups gluten-
   free plain/all-purpose
   baking flour plus 1
   teaspoon xanthan gum
50 g/½ cup plus
   3 tablespoons ground
   almonds
100 g/7 tablespoons
   butter, chilled and diced
100 g/½ cup cream cheese
50 g/¼ cup caster/
   superfine sugar
1 egg yolk
1 teaspoon pure vanilla
   extract
grated zest of 1 lemon

7.5-cm/3-in. cookie cutter
24 tartlet pans or 2 x
   12-hole muffin pans,
   greased
baking beans
piping/pastry bag, fitted
   with a large round
   nozzle/tip

MAKES 24

These dainty tartlets are the height of sophistication - crisp buttery pastry filled with real vanilla crème pâtissière and topped with glazed strawberries - they are the perfect accompaniment to a glass of chilled Champagne at a summer party.

To make the pastry, sift the flour into a mixing bowl and stir in the ground almonds. Rub in the butter until the mixture resembles fine breadcrumbs. Add the cream cheese, sugar, egg yolk, vanilla extract and lemon zest and mix to a soft dough with your fingers, adding a little water if the dough is too dry or extra flour if it is too sticky. Wrap in clingfilm/plastic wrap and chill for 1 hour.

Preheat the oven to 180°C (350°F) Gas 4. Dust a work surface with flour and use a rolling pin to roll out the pastry to a thickness of 3 mm/⅛ in. Stamp out 24 rounds with the cutter and press one into each prepared pan. Line the pastry cases with baking parchment, fill with baking beans and bake in the preheated oven for 12–15 minutes, until golden brown and crisp. Let cool on a wire rack.

To make the crème pâtissère, put the cornflour, sugar, egg and egg yolk in a bowl and whisk until creamy. Put the milk, cream and vanilla pod/bean in a saucepan and bring to the boil. Pour the hot milk over the egg mixture, whisking continuously. Return to the pan and cook for about 2 minutes, until thick. Remove the vanilla pod, pass the mixture through a sieve/strainer and let cool. Spoon the cooled crème pâtissière into the piping bag and fill the pastry cases. Arrange some strawberry halves on top. Put the preserve and lemon juice in a saucepan and heat until runny, pass through a sieve/strainer, let cool slightly, then brush over the top of each tartlet to glaze using a pastry brush.

These tartlets are best eaten on the day they are made.

Mini citrus meringue pies

60 g/½ cup plain/all-purpose flour, plus extra for dusting

1 tablespoon cocoa powder

60 g/½ stick butter, chilled and diced

25 g/2 tablespoons caster/granulated sugar

CITRUS CURD

80 ml/⅓ cup lemon juice (roughly 3 lemons)

60 g/½ stick butter

115 g/⅓ cup plus 1 tablespoon caster/superfine sugar

2 eggs, beaten

MERINGUE TOPPING

100 g/½ cup caster/superfine sugar

40 ml/2½ tablespoons golden syrup/light corn syrup

2 large egg whites

24 x 5-cm/2-in. fluted tartlet pans, greased

baking beans

piping/pastry bag fitted with a large star nozzle/tip

kitchen blowtorch (optional)

MAKES 24

These little pies are full of tangy citrus curd, topped with a fluffy meringue and encased in crisp chocolate shortcake.

To make the citrus curd, put the juice, butter and sugar in a heatproof bowl set over a pan of simmering water and whisk until the sugar has dissolved. Add the beaten eggs, whisking continuously, until the mixture thickens. Pass through a sieve/strainer to remove any lumps. Leave to cool, then store in the refrigerator until needed.

To make the pastry, sift the flour and cocoa powder into a mixing bowl and rub in the butter with your fingertips, until the mixture resembles fine breadcrumbs. Add the sugar, and a little cold water if the mixture is too dry, and work the pastry with your hands until it comes together into a ball. Wrap in clingfilm/plastic wrap and chill in the refrigerator for 1 hour.

Preheat the oven to 180°C (350°F) Gas 4.

On a flour-dusted surface, roll out the pastry to a thickness of about 3 mm/⅛ in. Cut out rounds of pastry slightly larger than the tart pans with a sharp knife. Press a round of pastry into each pan, trimming away any excess with a sharp knife. Transfer to the refrigerator for 30 minutes, then remove, line each pan with baking parchment and fill with baking beans. Bake in the preheated oven for 10–15 minutes, until the tarts cases are crisp. Turn out onto a wire rack and leave to cool. Fill each case with the citrus curd.

To make the meringue, heat the sugar, syrup and 2½ tablespoons water in a saucepan, until the sugar has dissolved and bring to the boil. Put the egg whites in a bowl and whisk to a stiff peak. Pour in the hot sugar syrup and whisk continuously until the meringue is cold. Spoon the meringue into the piping bag and pipe a swirl on top of the curd.

Lightly brown the meringue with a blowtorch or under a grill/broiler. Serve the pies immediately or store in the refrigerator until needed.

CHOUX & PUFF PASTRY

Peaches & cream choux rings with amaretti crumble topping

double quantity of Basic Choux Pastry (see page 153)

CRUMBLE TOPPING

70 g/2¾ oz. ratafia or amaretti biscuits/ cookies

50 g/1¾ oz. golden marzipan

50 g/3½ tablespoons butter, melted

FILLING

600 ml/2½ cups double/heavy cream

50 ml/scant ¼ cup amaretto or other almond liqueur

6 ripe peaches or nectarines, stoned/pitted and thinly sliced

icing/confectioners' sugar, for dusting

2 baking sheets lined with baking parchment or a silicon mat

2 piping/pastry bags fitted with large star nozzles/tips

MAKES 6

Summer on a plate! These choux rings are topped with an almond crumble which gives a great crunchy texture to the choux. If you are serving to children simply omit the alcohol.

Begin by making the crumble topping. Break the ratafia biscuits to very small pieces using your hands. Finely chop the marzipan and add with the warm melted butter to the ratafia. Crush the mixture together with your hands until you have large crumbs of the mixture.

Preheat the oven to 200°C (400°F) Gas 6.

Spoon the choux pastry into a piping bag and pipe 18 rings about 7 cm/ 3 in. in diameter onto the lined baking sheets, a small distance apart. Pat down any peaks in the pastry using a clean wet finger. Top each ring with a little of the crumble topping. Do not worry if any of the crumbs fall onto the baking sheet as these can be discarded after baking. Sprinkle a little water into the bottom of the oven to create steam which will help the choux pastry to rise.

Bake each baking sheet in the oven for 10 minutes, then reduce the oven temperature to 180°C (350°F) Gas 4 and bake for a further 15–20 minutes until the pastry is crisp. Watch that the crumble topping does not burn towards the end of cooking. Remove from the oven and cut a slit into each ring to allow any steam to escape. Leave to cool.

In a mixing bowl whisk together the cream and amaretto to stiff peaks. Spoon the cream into the second piping bag. Pipe a swirl of cream onto the buns. Top each with the fruit slices in pretty patterns and dust with icing sugar to serve. Store in the refrigerator if not serving straight away as they contain fresh cream. These are best eaten on the day they are made.

Fresh fruit éclairs

These éclairs are inspired by the elegant fresh fruit tarts that line the windows in French pâtisseries. They are simple to prepare and make a stunning addition to a summer afternoon tea.

Preheat the oven to 200°C (400°F) Gas 6.

Spoon the choux pastry into one of the piping bags and pipe 12 lengths of pastry, about 10 cm/4 in. long, onto the lined baking sheet, a small distance apart. Pat down any peaks in the pastry using a clean wet finger.

Sprinkle a little water into the bottom of the oven to create steam which will help the choux pastry to rise. Bake in the oven for 10 minutes, then reduce the oven temperature to 180°C (350°F) Gas 4 and bake for a further 15–20 minutes until the pastry is crisp. Remove from the oven and cut a small slit into each éclair to allow any steam to escape. Leave to cool.

The éclairs need to be filled with the cream before being decorated, as the decoration is fragile. Working in a cool place, make a small hole in the base of each éclair and pipe until full of cream.

For the topping, place the white chocolate in a heatproof bowl over a saucepan of water and simmer until the chocolate is melted. Leave for about 10 minutes so that the chocolate cools slightly and thickens. Using a knife, spread some white chocolate neatly over the top of each éclair. Place the small pieces fruit in decorative patterns on top of the chocolate. It is important to only use small pieces otherwise they will be too heavy and cause the éclairs to topple over. It is best to do this with the éclairs balanced in the grooves of a cooling rack.

Serve the éclairs straight away or store in the refrigerator until needed. The éclairs are best eaten on the day they are made, although can be eaten the following day if stored in the refrigerator.

1 quantity of Basic Choux Pastry (see page 153)

FILLING
300 ml/1¼ cups double/ heavy cream, whipped to stiff peaks

TOPPING
150 g/5½ oz. white chocolate

small pieces of fresh fruit of your choice (mango, grapes, raspberries and blueberries all work well)

2 piping/pastry bags fitted with round nozzles/tips

large baking sheet lined with baking parchment or a silicon mat

MAKES 12

Gluten-free nectarine & cream choux rings

50 g/½ cup flaked/sliced almonds

3 ripe nectarines, stoned/pitted and thickly sliced

125 ml/½ cup sweet dessert wine

1 tablespoon honey

1 teaspoon pure vanilla extract

250 ml/1 cup double/heavy cream

1 generous tablespoon icing/confectioners' sugar, plus extra for dusting

GLUTEN-FREE CHOUX PASTRY

65 g/½ cup gluten-free plain/all-purpose baking flour

50 g/3½ tablespoons butter

2 large/US extra-large eggs, beaten with 2 teaspoons pure vanilla extract

2 piping/pastry bags, 1 fitted with a large round nozzle/tip and the other fitted with a large star nozzle/tip

baking sheet, greased and lined with baking parchment

MAKES 12

These delicate light pastries, filled with dessert wine and honey-poached nectarines are a real treat in summer when the fruits are in season. You can substitute peaches or apricots in place of the nectarines if you prefer.

Preheat the oven to 200°C (400°F) Gas 6.

To make the choux buns, sift the flour twice to remove any lumps. Heat the butter in a saucepan with 150 ml/⅔ cup cold water, until the butter is melted. Bring to the boil, then shoot in the flour all in one go (very quickly) and remove from the heat. Beat hard with a wooden spoon until the dough forms a ball and no longer sticks to the sides of the pan. Leave to cool for about 5 minutes. Add the eggs a small amount at a time and use a balloon whisk to beat them into the dough. The mixture will form a sticky paste which holds its shape when you lift the whisk up.

Spoon the choux dough into the piping bag fitted with a round nozzle and pipe 12 rings of choux pastry onto the prepared baking sheet. With clean hands wet your finger and smooth down any peaks from the piping so that the pastry is smooth. Sprinkle with flaked almonds.

Bake in the preheated oven for 15 minutes, then use a sharp knife to puncture each ring to allow the steam to escape. Return them to the oven for a further 5 minutes, until crisp. Cool on a wire rack and then cut in half.

Put the nectarines in a saucepan with the wine, honey and vanilla extract. Simmer over gentle heat for 5 minutes. Leave to cool completely.

Whip the cream to stiff peaks, sift in the icing sugar and whisk in. Spoon the cream into the piping bag fitted with a star nozzle and pipe a ring of cream onto the base of each choux ring.

Drain the poached nectarines and cut into small pieces with a sharp knife. Arrange a few on top of the cream. Top with the remaining choux halves and dust with icing sugar. Serve immediately or cover and refrigerate until needed.

These choux rings are best eaten on the day they are made as they contain fresh cream.

Passion fruit eclairs

1 quantity of Basic Choux Pastry (see page 153)

180 g/6 oz. fondant icing/ confectioners' sugar, sifted

2–3 passion fruit, juiced and seeds removed

50 g/1¾ oz. plain/ semisweet chocolate, melted

CHOCOLATE MOUSSE

200 g/7 oz. plain/ semisweet chocolate

3 passion fruit, skins discarded

100 ml/scant ½ cup double/heavy cream

2 egg whites

20 g/4 teaspoons caster/ superfine sugar

baking sheet lined with baking parchment

2 piping/pastry bags fitted with large round nozzles/ tips

MAKES 12

Chocolate and passion fruit are a super modern combination – the tanginess of the summery fruit brings the chocolate to life.

Begin by preparing the chocolate mousse as it needs time to set. Place the chocolate in a heatproof bowl set over a pan of simmering water until it is all melted. Stir the passion fruit juice, flesh and seeds, and cream into the melted chocolate. The seeds of the passion fruit add a crunchy texture to these éclairs but if you are not keen on them, just remove them using a sieve/strainer and add the juice and flesh of the passion fruit to the chocolate mousse, leaving out the seeds. Whisk the egg whites to stiff peaks, then whisk in the sugar gradually. Fold the egg whites into the chocolate and leave to chill in the refrigerator for about 3 hours or overnight until the mousse is set.

Preheat the oven to 200°C (400°F) Gas 6.

Spoon the choux pastry into one of the piping bags and pipe 12 lines of pastry onto the baking sheet about 10 cm/4 in. in length, a small distance apart. Pat down any peaks in the pastry using a clean wet finger. Sprinkle a little water into the bottom of the oven to create steam which will help the choux pastry to rise.

Bake in the oven for 10 minutes, then reduce the oven temperature to 180°C (350°F) Gas 4 and bake for a further 15–20 minutes until the pastry is crisp. Remove from the oven and cut a small slit into each pastry to allow steam to escape. Leave to cool then cut the éclairs in half lengthways.

For the icing, mix the icing sugar with the passion fruit juice until smooth, adding a little water if it is too stiff. This will depend on how much juice was released from your fruit so add gradually. Spread the icing over the top of each éclair. Using a fork, drizzle thin lines of melted chocolate onto the icing and swirl in with a cocktail stick/toothpick before the icing sets.

When you are ready to serve, spoon the choux pastry into the other piping bag and pipe a line of the chocolate passion fruit mousse into the bottom of each éclair. Cover with the iced tops and serve straight away or store in the refrigerator until needed. The éclairs are best eaten on the day they are made, although can be eaten the following day if you wish.

Lemon meringue choux buns

1 quantity of Basic Choux Pastry (see page 153)

LEMON FILLING

200 g/7 oz. white chocolate

125 ml/½ cup double/heavy cream

2 tablespoons lemon curd

2 egg whites

2 tablespoons caster/superfine sugar

ICING

160 g/1⅓ cups icing/confectioners' sugar, sifted

freshly squeezed juice of 1 lemon

yellow food colouring (optional)

MERINGUE TOPPING

100 g/½ cup caster/superfine sugar

1 tablespoon golden/light corn syrup

2 egg whites

baking sheet lined with baking parchment

3 piping/pastry bags, 2 fitted with round nozzles/tips and 1 with a large star nozzle/tip

kitchen blowtorch

MAKES 14

Taking inspiration from the classic dessert lemon meringue pie, these dainty choux buns have a a sharp lemon icing and fluffy meringue.

Begin by preparing the lemon mousse as it needs to set before being used to fill the choux buns. Melt the white chocolate in a heatproof bowl set over a saucepan of water, stirring occasionally. Once melted, remove from the heat and leave to cool slightly. Add the cream and lemon curd to the bowl and mix together to form a smooth paste. In a separate bowl, whisk the egg whites to stiff peaks. While still whisking, add the sugar gradually until the meringue is glossy. Gently fold the white chocolate mixture into the meringue. Leave in the refrigerator to set, for at least 3 hours or preferably overnight.

Preheat the oven to 200°C (400°F) Gas 6.

Spoon the choux pastry into one of the piping bags fitted with a round nozzle and pipe 14 round balls onto the baking sheet, a small distance apart. Pat down any peaks in the pastry using a clean wet finger. Sprinkle a little water into the bottom of the oven to create steam. Bake in the oven for 10 minutes, then reduce the oven temperature to 180°C (350°F) Gas 4 and bake for a further 15–20 minutes until the pastry is crisp. Remove from the oven and cut a small slit into each pastry to allow steam to escape. Leave to cool then make a small hole in the base of each bun.

For the icing, mix together the icing sugar with enough lemon juice until you have a smooth thick icing. Add a few drops of yellow food colouring if you wish. Dip the tops of the buns into the icing, invert and leave on a rack to set.

For the meringue, heat the sugar, syrup and 60 ml/¼ cup water in a saucepan and bring to the boil. Whisk the egg whites to stiff peaks and then pour the hot syrup into the eggs, whisking all the time. It is best to do this with a stand mixer, or if you do not have one, have someone else pour the hot syrup in while you whisk. Whisk for about 5 minutes until the meringue is stiff and glossy.

Place the lemon mousse into the other piping bag fitted with a round nozzle and pipe the mousse into each bun so that they are full. Spoon the meringue into the piping bag fitted with the star nozzle and pipe a large star of meringue on top of each bun. Using the blowtorch, caramelize the meringue until lightly golden. The buns are best eaten on the day they are made.

1 quantity of Basic Choux
Pastry (see page 153)

FILLING
80 g/⅓ cup caster/
superfine sugar
1 teaspoon culinary
lavender buds
300 ml/1¼ cups
double/heavy cream

SAUCE & DECORATION
200 g/7 oz. cream-filled
white chocolate
(such as Lindor White)
or white chocolate
200 ml/generous ¾ cup
double/heavy cream
15 g/1 tablespoon butter
purple edible glitter
(optional)

2 baking sheets lined with
baking parchment
2 piping/pastry bags
fitted with large round
nozzles/tips
pestle and mortar
12 paper cases, to serve

MAKES 24

White chocolate & lavender profiteroles

Cooking with lavender in the height of summer is a real delight. These are not strictly summer fruits, but we couldn't pass up the opportunity to celebrate the beauty of lavender in these delicate profiteroles.

Preheat the oven to 200°C (400°F) Gas 6. Spoon the choux pastry into one of the piping bags and pipe 24 small balls of choux pastry onto the lined baking sheets. Pat down any peaks in the pastry using a clean wet finger. Sprinkle a little water into the bottom of the oven to create steam.

Bake each sheet in the oven for 10 minutes, then reduce the oven temperature to 180°C (350°F) Gas 4 and bake for a further 10–20 minutes until the pastry is crisp. Remove from the oven and cut a small slit into each with a sharp knife to let any steam escape. Leave to cool.

Place the sugar and 60 ml/¼ cup water into a saucepan and simmer until the sugar has dissolved, then bring to the boil. Grind the lavender using a pestle and mortar and add to the sugar syrup. Simmer for a minute then remove from the heat and leave to cool completely. When you are ready to serve whisk the double cream and lavender syrup together to stiff peaks. Make a small hole in the bottom of each profiterole, using a sharp knife. Spoon the cream into a piping bag and pipe into the profiteroles.

For the sauce, place the chocolate in a heatproof bowl set over a saucepan of water and simmer until the chocolate is melted. Add the cream and the butter and stir until melted.

Coat the profiteroles in the sauce and sprinkle with edible glitter, or serve with the sauce on the side either warm or cold. The profiteroles are best eaten on the day they are made, although can be eaten the following day if stored in the refrigerator.

Rose & raspberry choux rings

1 quantity of Basic Choux Pastry (see page 153)

ICING & DECORATION
150 g/5½ oz. fondant icing/confectioners' sugar, sifted
1 tablespoon rose syrup
pink food colouring
crystallized rose petals

FILLING
300 ml/1¼ cups double/heavy cream
1 tablespoon rose syrup
280 g/10 oz. raspberries

large baking sheet, lined with baking parchment or a silicon mat
2 piping/pastry bags, 1 fitted with a round and 1 with a star nozzle/tip
10 paper cases, to serve

MAKES 10

When raspberries are in season, these delicate choux rings are a perfect treat. With a rosy posy icing and crystallized rose petals, they make an elegant summer dessert bursting with tangy raspberries.

Preheat the oven to 200°C (400°F) Gas 6.

Spoon the choux pastry into the piping bag fitted with a round nozzle and pipe 10 rings of pastry, about 6 cm/2½ in. in diameter onto the baking sheet a small distance apart. Pat down any peaks in the pastry using a clean wet finger. Sprinkle a little water into the bottom of the oven to create steam which will help the choux pastry to rise.

Bake in the oven for 10 minutes, then reduce the oven temperature to 180°C (350°F) Gas 4 and bake for a further 15–20 minutes until the pastry is crisp. Remove from the oven and cut a small slit into each ring to allow any steam to escape and leave to cool. Carefully cut each ring in half horizontally using a sharp knife.

For the icing, mix the icing sugar with the rose syrup and a few drops of food colouring until you have a thick icing, adding a little water if needed. Spread a little icing over the tops of the choux rings. Decorate each top with some crystallized rose petals and then leave the icing to set.

Once the icing is set, whip the cream and rose syrup for the filling to stiff peaks then spoon into the piping bag fitted with a star nozzle. Pipe swirls of cream into the bottom of each ring. Top with fresh raspberries then place an iced ring on top of each one. Serve straight away or store in the refrigerator if you are not eating straight away. These choux buns are best eaten on the day they are made.

Strawberry choux ring

double quantity of
  Basic Choux Pastry
  (see page 153)
25 g/1 oz. flaked/sliced
  almonds

TO ASSEMBLE
500 ml/2 cups double/
  heavy cream
1 tablespoon icing/
  confectioners' sugar,
  sifted, plus extra for
  dusting
1 teaspoon vanilla bean
  paste or pure vanilla
  extract
400 g/14 oz. ripe
  strawberries
2–3 tablespoons
  strawberry jam/jelly

baking sheet lined with
  baking parchment or
  a silicon mat
2 piping/pastry bags,
  1 fitted with large round
  nozzle/tip and 1 with
  a large star nozzle/tip

SERVES 8

Filled with sweet Chantilly cream, ripe strawberries and strawberry jam with an extra crunch of almonds, this is a perfect summer's day dessert. If you prefer you can pipe small rings and make individual desserts.

Preheat the oven to 200°C (400°F) Gas 6.

Spoon the choux pastry into the piping bag fitted with a round nozzle and pipe large balls of the choux pastry in a ring about 22 cm/9 in. in diameter on the lined baking sheet. Pat down any peaks in the pastry using a clean wet finger. Sprinkle the top of the ring with the flaked almonds. Then sprinkle a little water into the bottom of the oven to create steam which will help the choux pastry to rise.

Bake in the oven for 20 minutes, then reduce the oven temperature to 180°C (350°F) Gas 4 and bake for a further 25 minutes until the pastry is crisp. Remove from the oven and cut a few slits into the ring using a sharp knife to allow any steam to escape, then return to the oven for a further 5 minutes. Remove from the oven and leave to cool.

Once cool, cut the ring in half horizontally using a large serrated knife. The ring is fragile so you need to cut carefully. Do not worry too much if the top of the ring breaks as you can sandwich it back together with the cream filling.

Place the cream, icing sugar and vanilla bean paste in a mixing bowl and whisk to stiff peaks. Spoon the cream into the piping bag fitted with the star nozzle and pipe swirls of cream onto the bottom of each choux ball in the ring around the outside edge, reserving a little cream to decorate the top.

Reserve a few strawberries for decoration, then hull the remaining strawberries and cut into halves. Place the halved strawberries on top of the cream and top with small teaspoons of strawberry jam. Carefully lift and place the almond-topped choux ring on top of the cream and strawberries. Dust with icing sugar and then pipe small stars of cream on top of the ring before carefully placing the reserved strawberries on top.

Serve straight away or store in the refrigerator until needed. This is best eaten on the day it is made, although can be eaten the following day if you wish.

Plum pithiviers

1 quantity of Frangipane
   (see page 156)
150 g/5½ oz. plums,
   stoned/pitted and
   quartered
100 g/scant ½ cup plum
   jam/jelly
375 g/13 oz. storebought
   all-butter puff pastry
   (thawed if frozen)
plain/all-purpose flour,
   for dusting
1 teaspoon mixed spice/
   apple pie spice
1 egg, lightly beaten,
   to glaze

10-cm/4-in. round cookie
   cutter
12-cm/5-in. round cookie
   cutter
baking sheet, lined with
   baking parchment
piping/pastry bag fitted
   with a plain nozzle/tip

MAKES 4–6

This recipe is so straightforward - two discs of puff pastry filled with sweet frangipane - can be sweet or savoury and is often made as one large tart. Be warned that pithiviers can take a bit of time to make perfectly, but they always wow guests.

Make the frangipane following the instructions on page 156, then refrigerate to set while you continue with the recipe. Put the plums and jam in a saucepan over medium heat and warm just until the plums are beginning to cook and break down. Do not be tempted to cook it for too long as you still want some texture in there. Allow to cool slightly.

Using a rolling pin, roll out the puff pastry on a lightly floured surface until about 7 mm/⅓ in. thick. Stamp out 4–6 rounds using the smaller cookie cutter, and the same number using the larger cookie cutter. Arrange the rounds on the prepared baking sheet.

Spoon or pipe a little of the frangipane onto the smaller pastry rounds. These will be the bases of the pithiviers. Leave a 1-cm/½-in. border around the edge. You need to reserve the same amount of frangipane for later.

Put a teaspoonful of the cooled plum compote onto the frangipane. Now top with the remaining frangipane so that the blob of compote is encased in frangipane. Place the larger rounds of pastry on top of the frangipane and seal by pressing the tines of a fork around the edges.

To make the distinctive pattern on the pastry tops, take a very sharp knife and score curved lines on them, from the middle to the edge, all the way around.

Brush the beaten egg over the pithiviers to glaze them. Bake in the preheated oven for 20 minutes or until puffed up and golden.

Puff pastry strawberry ring

500 g/1 lb. 2 oz.
storebought all-butter
puff pastry (thawed if
frozen)

1 large/US extra-large egg,
beaten

1 tablespoon caster/
superfine sugar

300 ml/1¼ cups double/
heavy cream

2 tablespoons icing/
confectioners' sugar

seeds of ½ vanilla
pod/bean or 1 teaspoon
pure vanilla extract

400 g/14 oz. strawberries,
hulled and sliced

plain/all-purpose flour,
for dusting

icing/confectioners'
sugar for dusting

*large baking sheet
(or 2 smaller baking
sheets), lined with
silicon mats or baking
parchment*

*8-cm/3-in. round
cookie cutter*

SERVES 6

This dessert looks spectacular, similar to the French classic croquembouche, but is actually far simpler to prepare and tastes light and delicious. If you prefer, you can make small individual portions, or for a special celebration, you can increase the number of puff pastry rings and make a giant tower instead.

Preheat the oven to 200°C (400°F) Gas 6.

On a flour-dusted surface, roll out the pastry very thinly into a large rectangle using a rolling pin. Cut out one large disc of pastry using a 25-cm/10-in. plate as a template, cutting round it with a sharp knife. Using the rolling pin to help lift, transfer the pastry disc to the baking sheet. Next, cut out two smaller discs of pastry using 14-cm/5½-in. and 18-cm/7-in. plates as templates. Transfer both discs of pastry to the baking sheet(s) and cut a hole in the centre of each of the two smaller pastry discs using the 8-cm/3-in. round cutter. Discard one of the cut-out circles and place the other on the baking sheet(s). (You should have 25-cm/10-in. and 8-cm/3-in. round discs of pastry and 14-cm/5½-in. and 18-cm/7-in. rings.)

Brush the top of the pastry with a little of the beaten egg using a pastry brush and sprinkle with a little caster/granulated sugar. Bake in the preheated oven for 25–30 minutes until the pastry is crisp and golden brown and has risen. Leave on the baking sheet(s) to cool. When you are ready to serve, in a clean mixing bowl, whisk the double/heavy cream, icing/confectioners' sugar and vanilla together to stiff peaks.

Place the largest disc of pastry on your serving plate and spread about half of the cream over and cover with some of the strawberry slices. Carefully spread a little cream around the top of the largest ring of pastry (taking care as it is fragile) and then place on top of the strawberry-covered disc. Decorate with strawberries. Repeat these steps with the smaller ring. Top the ring with cream and strawberries and place the small pastry disc on top.

Dust the whole cake with icing sugar and serve immediately, cutting the cake into slices with a sharp knife. The cake is best eaten on the day it is assembled although you can cook the pastry the day before if you wish.

Napoleon cakes

400 g/14 oz. storebought all-butter puff pastry (thawed if frozen)

2–3 tablespoons icing/ confectioners' sugar

FILLING

300 ml/1⅓ cups whipping cream

1 teaspoon icing/ confectioners' sugar

a drop of pure vanilla extract

½ quantity Crème Pâtissière (see page 154)

4–6 tablespoons raspberry jam/jelly

200–250 g/7–9 oz. raspberries

50 g/½ cup pistachio nuts

2 baking sheets,
1 greased and lined
with baking parchment
piping/pastry bag

MAKES 5

Napoleon cakes are essentially a variant of millefeuille. Many countries have variations that differ slightly in ingredients. The Swedish version is said to have been brought from Austria in 1876 – when a baker started Broqvist Bakery in Växjö.

Preheat the oven to 180°C (350°F) Gas 4.

Roll out the puff pastry to 35 x 30 cm/14 x 12 in. and transfer to the prepared baking sheet. Prick the top of the pastry with a fork and dust over the sugar. Put a piece of baking parchment on top of the pastry and then put the other baking sheet on top of that. This will prevent the pastry from rising when baking.

Bake in the preheated oven for around 15–16 minutes and then a further 3–4 minutes uncovered to give it a bit of colour.

Cut the pastry into two perfectly equal rectangles. Cut each rectangle into slices – depending on the size your pastry you will likely get ten slices. Leave to cool.

For the filling, whip the cream with the icing sugar and vanilla. Mix the cream with the crème pâtissière and fold well. It is essential that all of the ingredients are cold or it may spread out when you assemble the cake.

To assemble, spread the raspberry jam evenly across 5 of the slices, then carefully, using a piping bag, pipe the cream filling through the middle of each piece – followed by blobs along the edge alternating with raspberries. You want to make sure there is enough cream in there to balance the bases, but not so much that it overpowers.

Add a top layer to each and pipe more cream filling and decorate with more berries and slivers of pistachio nuts.

Pineapple & coconut millefeuilles

500 g/1 lb. 2 oz. storebought all-butter puff pastry (thawed if frozen)

1 large/US extra-large egg, beaten

plain/all-purpose flour, for dusting

caster/superfine sugar, for dusting

PINEAPPLE COMPOTE & GRIDDLED PINEAPPLE

1 large ripe pineapple, peeled and eyes removed

60 ml/¼ cup coconut rum

60 g/5 tablespoons caster/superfine sugar, plus extra for sprinkling

COCONUT CREAM

450 ml/generous 1¾ cups double/heavy cream

70 ml/generous ¼ cup coconut rum

1 tablespoon icing/confectioners' sugar, sifted, plus extra for dusting

3 large baking sheets, lined with baking parchment

piping/pastry bag fitted with a large star nozzle/tip

MAKES 6

This Caribbean-inspired millefeuille is truly delicious, featuring crisp glazed pastry filled with coconut rum cream, pineapple compote and caramelized pineapple slices for a taste of a tropical summer holiday.

Preheat the oven to 200°C (400°F) Gas 6.

On a flour-dusted surface, roll out the pastry to a 36-cm/14-in. square. Brush the top with a little beaten egg and sprinkle with a little caster sugar. Cut into three long equal strips. Place one of the pastry strips on one of the lined baking sheets and cover with baking parchment. Place a second lined baking sheet on top and place the two remaining pastry slices on top. Again cover with baking parchment and place the third baking sheet on top. (If you do not have 3 baking sheets you can cook the pastry in batches. However, placing the sheets on top prevents the pastry from rising too much and losing its shape.)

Bake for 40–50 minutes in the preheated oven until the pastry is golden brown and cooked all the way through. Leave to cool.

Thinly slice half of the pineapple into 12 slices. Core the remaining pineapple and chop the flesh into small pieces. Place the chopped flesh in a saucepan with the 60 ml/¼ cup coconut rum, 60 ml/¼ cup water and the sugar and simmer for about 10 minutes until soft. Blitz to a smooth purée in a blender then set aside to cool.

Heat a griddle pan until very hot and sprinkle the pineapple slices with a little caster sugar on both sides. Griddle them for 5 minutes on each side or until caramelized. Remove from the heat and leave to cool.

For the coconut cream, place the double cream and coconut rum in a mixing bowl with the icing sugar and whisk to stiff peaks. Spoon into the piping bag.

When you are ready to assemble, trim the edges of the pastry and cut each slice into six equal rectangles. Pipe small stars of cream around the edge of two-thirds of the pastry slices, leaving a gap in the middle. Fill the gaps with a teaspoon of the pineapple purée.

Assemble the pastry stacks by placing two cream-topped slices on top of each other, each time topping the cream with a griddled slice of pineapple. Top with a plain pastry slice and dust with icing sugar. Repeat with the remaining slices. Serve straight away or store in the refrigerator until needed.

Mango & coconut millefeuilles

375 g/13 oz. shopbought all-butter puff pastry (thawed if frozen)

100 g/⅓ cup icing/confectioners' sugar

COCONUT CRÈME PÂTISSIÈRE

200 ml/¾ cup whole milk

150 ml/⅔ cup coconut milk

½ vanilla pod/bean

3 egg yolks

50 g/¼ cup caster/superfine sugar

1½ tablespoons cornflour/cornstarch

1–2 tablespoons Malibu (optional)

MACERATED MANGO

1 large or 2 small ripe mangoes, peeled, stoned and flesh cut into small dice

zest and juice of 1 lime

2 baking sheets lined with baking parchment

disposable piping/pastry bag

MAKES 12

Mango really benefits from a dressing of lime juice and it is paired here with a coconut crème pâtissière for a summery tropical feel.

Preheat the oven to 200°C (400°F) Gas 6.

Cut the pastry into three evenly sized pieces. Roll each piece out on a lightly floured work surface into neat 18 x 23-cm/7 x 9-in. rectangles. Lay clingfilm/plastic wrap on top of each one and stack on top of a floured baking sheet. Chill in the fridge for 20 minutes until firm.

Transfer one of the rectangles to one of the lined baking sheets. Dust with icing sugar and lay a sheet of baking parchment on top. Place an unlined baking sheet directly on top of the parchment and bake on the middle shelf of the preheated oven for about 12 minutes until the pastry is golden brown, crisp and caramelized on top. Bake the other pastry rectangles in the same way. Leave to cool, then, using a serrated knife, cut each rectangle into 7 x 4-cm/3 x 1½-in. rectangles – you need 36.

To make the crème pâtissière, heat the milk with the coconut milk and vanilla pod in a small pan over low heat. Bring slowly just to the boil, then remove from the heat and leave to infuse for 15 minutes. Meanwhile beat the egg yolks with the caster sugar and cornflour until pale and light. Remove the vanilla pod and reheat the vanilla-infused milk until just below boiling, then, whisking constantly, pour into the bowl with the egg mixture. Mix until smooth, then return to the pan and, stirring constantly, heat over low–medium heat until gently boiling and thickened. Add the Malibu, if using, and mix in. Strain the mixture through a fine mesh sieve/strainer into a bowl and cover the surface with clingfilm/plastic wrap to prevent a skin forming. Leave until cold.

Tip the mango into a bowl, add the lime zest and juice, mix to combine and macerate for 30 minutes.

Lay 24 of the pastry rectangles on the work surface – keep the best looking 12 for the tops. Drain the mango. Scoop the crème pâtissière into the piping bag and pipe small bulbs at each corner of all 24 rectangles. Place a few pieces of mango alongside the crème and continue piping crème, alternated with mango, until the surface of each rectangle is covered like a chequerboard. Carefully place 12 garnished pastries on a serving plate and top with a second layer. Position the reserved pastry rectangles on top and serve.

FRUIT-FILLED
TARTS & PIES

Pineapple & star anise tartes tatin

140 g/scant ¾ cup caster/
  superfine sugar, plus
  extra for sprinkling
80 g/¾ stick butter
a pinch of salt
1 ripe pineapple
8 star anise
500 g/1 lb. 2 oz.
  storebought puff pastry
  (thawed if frozen)
plain/all-purpose flour,
  for dusting
milk, for brushing
whipped cream flavoured
  with coconut rum,
  to serve (optional)

2 x 4-hole Yorkshire
  pudding pans (with
  10-cm/4-in. holes),
  greased, or 8 x
  10-cm/4-in. mini tatin
  pans, greased
10-cm/4-in. round cookie
  cutter

MAKES 8

While tartes tatin are traditionally made with apples, pineapple also works brilliantly. It releases its golden juices into the caramel on cooking, which gives it a distinctly tropical flavour. The star anise, although not edible, imparts a delicate hint of aniseed into the caramel as well.

In a heavy-based saucepan, heat the sugar until it melts and turns golden brown. Do not stir, but swirl the pan to prevent the sugar from burning. Watch closely as the sugar melts, as it can easily burn. Once caramelized, add the butter and salt to the pan, whisking as it melts to make a caramel sauce. Divide the caramel equally between the holes of the Yorkshire pudding pans or mini tatin pans and leave to cool.

Peel and core the pineapple and cut into 8 rings. (If you are short of time you can use tinned/canned pineapple instead.) Place a pineapple ring into each hole and press a star anise into the centre of each one.

Preheat the oven to 200°C (400°F) Gas 6.

On a flour-dusted surface, roll the pastry thinly and cut out 8 discs of pastry using a 10-cm/4-in. round cutter. If you do not have a large enough cookie cutter, use a small plate or bowl as a template to cut round, using a sharp knife.

Press the pastry tightly over the pineapple, crimping around the edges. Brush the pastry with a little milk to glaze and sprinkle with a little sugar.

Bake in the preheated oven for 15–20 minutes, until the pastry has risen and is golden brown. Remove from the oven, allow to cool for a few minutes, then carefully invert the pans onto a tray, taking care that you do not burn yourself on the hot caramel.

Serve immediately, with whipped cream flavoured with coconut rum if you wish. The star anise are for flavouring purposes only and should not be eaten. These tarts are best eaten on the day they are made.

Fresh apricot tart

PASTRY

175 g/1½ sticks butter, softened

50 g/¼ cup caster/superfine sugar

a pinch of salt

1 egg yolk

250 g/2 cups plain/all-purpose flour

FILLING

120 g/1 stick butter, softened

a pinch of salt

120 g/⅔ cup caster/superfine sugar

2 eggs

120 g/1 cup ground almonds/almond meal

750 g/1 lb. 10 oz. fresh, ripe (but firm) apricots, quartered and stoned/pitted

5 tablespoons smooth apricot jam/jelly

23-cm/9-in. tart pan with removable base

baking beans

SERVES 6–8

Apricots are only briefly in season, so it's best to use them early summer to inject a splash of sunshine to any meal.

Preheat the oven to 180°C (350°F) Gas 4.

For the pastry, beat the butter, sugar and salt together until smooth. Add the egg yolk and stir until thoroughly mixed. Fold in the flour and bring it all together to form a smooth dough. Wrap in clingfilm/plastic wrap and set aside in a cool place while preparing the filling.

For the filling, beat the butter, salt and sugar together until light and fluffy. Stir in the eggs and beat until fully combined. Add the almonds and stir until they are fully incorporated and the mixture is smooth.

Roll out the pastry and use it to line the tart pan. Trim off the excess. Line the pan with the pastry and trim off the excess. Line with baking parchment, fill with baking beans and bake the pastry blind for about 10 minutes, or until light golden and firm. Allow to cool.

Spread the filling in an even layer over the tart base. Arrange the apricots over the filling, facing up in concentric circles and close together. Bake the tart for about 45 minutes, until the filling is firm and golden. Remove from the oven and allow to cool. Finally, warm the apricot jam with 1 tablespoon water and brush it all over the apricots for a shiny glaze.

Rhubarb & mascarpone tart

FILLING
500 g/1 lb. 2 oz. rhubarb, cut into 2.5-cm/1-in. slices

175 g/¾ cup caster/superfine sugar

30 g/2 tablespoons salted butter, softened

225 g/scant 1 cup mascarpone

30 g/¼ cup plain/all-purpose flour

grated zest of 1 orange

2 eggs, separated

100 ml/scant ½ cup double/heavy cream

SHORTBREAD BASE
135 g/1 stick plus 2 tablespoons salted butter, softened

65 g/⅓ cup caster/superfine sugar

160 g/1¼ cups plain/all-purpose flour

15 g/2 tablespoons cornflour/cornstarch

25 g/3 tablespoons rice flour

SYRUP
2 teaspoons arrowroot

freshly squeezed juice of 1 orange

23-cm/9-in. loose-based tart pan

baking beans

SERVES 8–10

Few things can compete with the first cut of outdoor-grown rhubarb every season – the pleasing sharpness of the fruit contrasts wonderfully well with the creamy mascarpone filling in this tart.

Preheat the oven to 190°C (375°F) Gas 5.

Put the rhubarb for the filling in an ovenproof dish, sprinkle 60 g/⅓ cup of the sugar over the top and cover with foil. Roast in the preheated oven for about 15 minutes. Remove the rhubarb from the oven and strain it, reserving the juice for later. Set aside. Leave the oven on.

To make the shortbread base, put all the ingredients in a large bowl and rub together using your fingertips until it forms a paste. Knead gently into a smooth ball of dough (refrigerate it for a few minutes if it is too soft to work). Roll out the pastry on a lightly floured surface to form a circle about 5 cm/ 2 in. larger than the pan. Drape the pastry over the rolling pin and carefully transfer it to the tart pan. Gently mould the pastry into the base and sides. Trim the top edge with a sharp knife. Line the tart case with a sheet of baking parchment. Fill the tart case with baking beans and blind bake for 15–20 minutes. Take out of the oven, remove the parchment and baking beans. When cool, line the sides of the tart pan with strips of baking parchment about 5 cm/2 in. high.

To make the filling, put the butter, remaining sugar, the mascarpone, flour and orange zest into a large bowl. Beat until evenly mixed, then add the egg yolks and cream. Beat to a creamy consistency and set aside.

Put the egg whites in a clean, grease-free bowl and, using an electric stand mixer or hand whisk, whisk the egg whites on high speed until soft peaks are formed. Transfer to the mascarpone mixture and whisk together, then spoon into the tart case. Distribute the roasted rhubarb evenly over the filling. Bake for 40–45 minutes or until golden brown and the filling is set like a hot soufflé – firm but with a slight wobble!

To make the syrup, stir together the arrowroot and 2 tablespoons water in a cup. Put the reserved rhubarb juice and the orange juice into a saucepan and bring to the boil. Remove from the heat and start stirring in the arrowroot – it may not all be needed, depending on how much juice you've produced from your rhubarb. The syrup should be just slightly thickened, as it thickens further with cooling.

Serve the tart warm with the syrup poured on top.

Summer berry tart

SWEET SHORTCRUST PASTRY

200 g/1¾ sticks butter, chilled and diced

350 g/2⅔ cups plain/ all-purpose flour

125 g/¾ cup plus 2 tablespoons icing/ confectioners' sugar

1 teaspoon pure vanilla extract or seeds from ½ vanilla pod/bean

1 egg

PASTRY CREAM

1 egg yolk

1 egg

30 g/generous ¼ cup cornflour/cornstarch

80 g/⅓ cup plus 1 tablespoon caster/ superfine sugar

¼ teaspoon salt

500 ml/2 cups full-fat/ whole milk

seeds from 1 vanilla pod/ bean

25 g/1¾ tablespoons butter

TOPPING

600 g/1¼ lb. mixed summer berries such as blackberries, blueberries, wild strawberries, raspberries, cherries or redcurrants

food-safe flowers, to decorate (optional)

25-cm/10-in. loose-based tart pan

baking beans

SERVES 8

The beauty of this tart is in the topping – it showcases everything there is to love about the summer: berries, sunshine and the abundance of everything fresh.

To make the pastry, rub the cold butter into the flour until sandy in texture, then mix in the icing sugar and vanilla. Add the egg and mix until the dough is smooth and holds together, taking care not to over-mix. You can also make the dough by pulsing the ingredients together briefly in a food processor, if you like. Roll the dough into a ball, then wrap in clingfilm/plastic wrap and chill for at least 30 minutes before using.

For the pastry cream, whisk together the egg yolk and egg, cornflour, sugar and salt until well combined and set aside. Heat the milk and vanilla seeds until just boiling in a saucepan. Slowly pour one third of the milk into the egg and cornflour mixture, while whisking vigorously to incorporate but not scramble the eggs. Pour the egg mixture back into the saucepan with the rest of the milk. Whisk continuously and bring to the boil again for around 30 seconds until thickened. Remove from the heat and stir in the butter until melted. Pour into a bowl and leave to cool with a layer of baking parchment on top to prevent a skin from forming. Refrigerate, ideally for a few hours, before using. (This pastry cream will keep well in the refrigerator for a few days, if you want to make it in advance).

Preheat the oven to 175°C (350°F) Gas 4.

On a lightly floured surface, roll out the pastry to 5 mm/¼-in. thick. Carefully transfer to the tart pan. Let the edges hang over (you can trim those after baking). Ensure the pastry is snug in all the curves of the pan, then prick the bottom with a fork all over. Line with baking parchment and baking beans and bake blind in the preheated oven for around 15–20 minutes until golden all over and cooked through. Remove from oven and leave to cool.

Once completely cool, use a sharp knife to trim away any untidy edges while still in the pan. Remove from the tart pan and spread with a generous layer of cold pastry cream. Pile the centre of the tart with fresh berries. Decorate with food-safe flowers, if you like.

Apricot tart with mazarin

1 quantity of Sweet
Shortcrust Pastry
(see page 86)
crème fraîche or sour
cream, to serve
(optional)

MARZIPAN
200 g/2 cups finely
ground almonds
100 g/½ cup caster/
superfine sugar
100 g/scant ¾ cup icing/
confectioners' sugar
1 teaspoon almond extract
1 egg white, ideally
pasteurized

MAZARIN
150 g/5½ oz. marzipan
(see recipe above
or storebought 50%
almond content), grated
100 g/½ cup caster/
superfine sugar
100 g/7 tablespoons
butter, softened
2 eggs
50 g/generous ⅓ cup
plain/all-purpose flour
a pinch of salt

TO ASSEMBLE
10 ripe fresh apricots
½ teaspoon ground
cardamom
½ teaspoon ground
cinnamon
icing/confectioners' sugar,
for dusting

*36 x 13 cm/14 x 5 in.
rectangular tart pan,
greased*

SERVES 8–10

Apricots are delicious when combined with a little spice, so this tart pairs the delicious summer fruit with cardamom and cinnamon, but omit these if you prefer.

If making your own marzipan, first re-grind the ground almonds a few times if they feel coarse, as they should be very fine in texture. Blend all the ingredients together in a food processor until smooth. Roll the mixture into a log and wrap tightly in clingfilm/plastic wrap. Chill in the refrigerator for at least 1 hour before using.

Roll out the pastry on a lightly floured surface to a thickness of around 5 mm/¼-in. Carefully transfer to line the tart pan and let the edges hang over (you can trim those after baking). Ensure the pastry is snug in all the curves of the pan and refrigerate until ready to bake. Freeze any excess pastry for use in another recipe.

Preheat the oven to 180°C (350°F) Gas 4.

To make the mazarin, mix the together the marzipan and sugar until combined, using a stand mixer with the paddle attachment or a wooden spoon, then add the softened butter. Mix again until smooth then add the eggs, one by one, ensuring they are well incorporated.

Sift in the flour and salt and fold into the mixture.

Spoon out the mazarin onto the pastry base and spread out evenly. Cut the apricots in half and remove the stones/pits. Arrange the apricot halves evenly across the top of the mazarin. Add a dusting of cardamom and cinnamon and bake the tart in the preheated oven for 45–50 minutes or until the pastry is nicely browned at the edges and the mazarin has set.

Remove from the oven and allow to cool before trimming away any untidy pastry edges and removing from the pan. Dust with icing/confectioners' sugar and cut into slices. Serve with crème fraîche or sour cream on the side, if you like.

Glazed French fruit tart

PASTRY

115 g/1 stick butter, chilled and diced

280 g/generous 2 cups plain/all-purpose flour, sifted, plus extra for dusting

a pinch of salt

grated zest of 1 orange

FILLING

100 g/3½ oz. plain/semisweet chocolate, melted

250 g/generous 1 cup mascarpone cheese

300 ml/1¼ cups crème fraîche

2 heaped tablespoons icing/confectioners' sugar, sifted

½ teaspoon vanilla bean powder or 1 teaspoon pure vanilla extract

TO DECORATE

fresh berries of your choosing

1 packet glaze topping/fixing gel, such as Dr Oetker's (or 3 tablespoons apricot glaze)

1 teaspoon pure vanilla extract

1 tablespoon Grand Marnier or orange liqueur

23-cm/9-in. loose-bottom, fluted tart pan, greased

baking beans

SERVES 8–10

You can decorate this tart with any fruit of your choosing – red and black summer berries are perfect – even wild strawberries, if you are lucky enough to find them.

For the pastry, rub the butter into the flour and salt using your fingertips. Add the orange zest and 1 tablespoon of cold water, and mix in with a round-bladed knife, adding a little more water if the mixture is too dry. Wrap the pastry in clingfilm/plastic wrap and chill in the refrigerator for 30 minutes.

On a flour-dusted surface, roll out the pastry thinly into a circle just larger than the size of your tart pan. Using the rolling pin to help lift it, carefully move the pastry into the pan and press it down so that it fits snugly. Trim away any excess pastry using a sharp knife, but leave some pastry hanging over the edge of the pan. This will be trimmed neatly after the tart is baked. Prick the base with a fork and chill in the refrigerator for 30 minutes.

Preheat the oven to 200°C (400°F) Gas 6.

Line the pastry with baking parchment and fill with baking beans. Bake the pastry for 20–25 minutes, until lightly golden brown and crisp, then remove from the oven and let cool. When cool enough to handle, remove the baking beans and parchment. Trim the edge of the pastry by running a sharp knife along the edge of the pan.

Spread the melted chocolate over the base of the cooled pastry case.

For the filling, whisk together the mascarpone, crème fraîche, icing sugar and vanilla until smooth and creamy. Spoon into the tart case and spread out evenly. Decorate the top of the tart with fresh berries, arranging them so that all of the cream is covered.

To glaze, prepare the glaze topping/fixing gel according to the packet instructions, adding the vanilla extract and Grand Marnier to the mixture with the water. Leave until just cool, then spoon over the fruit. If you are using apricot glaze instead, heat it in a saucepan with the Grand Marnier and vanilla, let cool slightly and then brush in a thick layer over the tart to glaze using a pastry brush.

Allow to cool before serving. This tart can be kept for up to 2 days in the refrigerator, but is best eaten on the day it is made.

Rustic plum tart

500 g/1 lb. 2 oz. storebought all-butter puff pastry (thawed if frozen)

plain/all-purpose flour, for dusting

1 egg, beaten

FILLING

100 g/3½ oz. golden marzipan

100 g/1 cup ground almonds

50 g/¼ cup caster/ superfine sugar, plus extra to sprinkle

about 16–18 plums, stoned/ pitted and quartered

GLAZE

2 tablespoons apricot glaze or apricot jam/jelly

20-cm/8-in. square, loose-bottom, fluted tart pan, greased

SERVES 6–8

You could use a few different varieties of summer plums to create a decorative coloured pattern on this delicious tart if you wish.

Preheat the oven to 200°C (400°F) Gas 6.

On a flour-dusted surface, roll out the pastry thinly into a square using a rolling pin until it is about 6 cm/2¼ in. larger than the size of your pan. Using the rolling pin to help lift, carefully move the pastry into the pan and press it down so that it fits tightly into the corners of the pan. Brush the inside of the pastry case with some of the beaten egg using a pastry brush. This will help prevent the pastry becoming soggy. Grate the marzipan coarsely and then lightly stir in the ground almonds and sugar. Sprinkle the almond mixture into the pastry case in an even layer.

Place the plum quarters in rows in the pan in a decorative pattern. Pull the pastry edges up around the side of the plums. Brush the pastry with the remaining egg and sprinkle the fruit and pastry with a little extra sugar.

Bake the tart in the preheated oven for 30–40 minutes, until the pastry has puffed up and is golden brown and the fruit still holds its shape but has released some of its juices. Remove from the oven.

Heat the apricot glaze or jam in a saucepan and then brush over the warm plums to glaze. Serve immediately if you want to eat warm, but this tart is also nice served cold with whipped cream. It will keep for up to 2 days in an airtight container.

Tarte exotique

1 quantity of **Pâte Sablée**
  (see page 150)
3 tablespoons **Malibu rum**
1 quantity of **Mango and**
  Passion Fruit Crème
  Pâtissière (see page 154)
tropical or colourful fruits
  of your choice, eg
  mango, kiwi, papaya,
  figs, starfruit, physalis,
  passion fruit, pineapple,
  cut into chunks if large

20-cm/8-in. fluted tart pan,
  greased and lightly
  dusted with flour
baking beans

SERVES 6–8

This is a showpiece! Go all out with the tropical fruit, which nestle on an unexpected base of tropical crème pâtissière, bursting with flavour.

Preheat the oven to 180°C (350°F) Gas 4.

Take the pâte sablée out of the refrigerator and put on a lightly floured surface. Using a rolling pin, roll it out to a rough circle at about 25 cm/10 in. in diameter.

Loosely wrap the dough around the rolling pin and transfer it to the prepared tart pan. Unravel the dough into the pan. Gently coax the dough neatly into the curves and angles of the pan, press lightly into the sides and cut off any excess with a small, sharp knife.

Lay a sheet of baking parchment over the pan and fill it with baking beans. Put the pan on a baking sheet and bake in the preheated oven for about 10–15 minutes.

Lower the oven temperature to 160°C (325°F) Gas 3. Remove the paper and beans from the tart pan and return the tart case to the oven for 5–10 minutes.

Remove the tart case from the oven and allow to cool completely, then remove from the pan.

Stir the rum through the prepared crème pâtissière in a mixing bowl. Spoon the flavoured cream into the tart case and spread level with a spatula. Pile the fruit up in the tart case, any way you like!

Free-form caramelized peach tart

500 g/1 lb. 2 oz.
  storebought all-butter
  puff pastry (thawed if
  frozen)
4–6 ripe peaches
55 g/½ stick butter
freshly squeezed juice
  of ½ lemon
150 g/¾ cup caster/
  superfine sugar
whipped cream or crème
  fraîche, to serve

*a dinner plate,
  28 cm/11 in. diameter
  (to use as a template)*

SERVES 6

So simple to make with storebought pasrty and so good when peaches
are at their very best.

Preheat the oven to 230°C (450°F) Gas 8.

Roll out the pastry on a lightly floured work surface and cut out a circle,
28 cm/11 in. diameter, using a large dinner plate as a template. Lift onto
a baking sheet and make an edge by twisting the pastry over itself all the
way around the edge. Press lightly to seal. Still on the baking sheet, chill
or freeze for at least 15 minutes.

Peel the peaches if necessary, then halve and stone/pit them and cut into
chunky slices. Put the butter into a saucepan, then add the lemon juice
and half the sugar. Heat until melted, then add the peaches and toss
gently. Pile the peaches all over the pastry in a casual way. Sprinkle with
the remaining sugar and bake in the preheated oven for 20–25 minutes
until golden, puffed and caramelized.

Serve with whipped cream or crème fraîche.

Fresh fruit tart

1 storebought pre-baked
   sweet pastry tart shell

PASTRY CREAM
500 ml/2 cups full-fat/
   whole milk (or half milk
   and half cream)
1 vanilla pod/bean, split
5 egg yolks
50 g/¼ cup caster/
   superfine sugar
50 g/⅓ cup plain/
   all-purpose flour

FRUIT FILLING
1 small punnet
   blackberries
1 small punnet blueberries
1 small punnet
   strawberries
1 peach, thinly sliced
1 nectarine, thinly sliced
2 purple plums,
   thinly sliced
1 kiwi fruit, peeled, halved
   and thinly sliced
about 150 g/5½ oz. apricot
   jam/jelly

baking beans
27-cm/10½-in. loose-based
   tart pan, greased and
   floured

SERVES 8–10

In French pastry shops, this tart is often made in a more orderly fashion, with all the fruit arranged in neat circles, but feel free to take the easier, more higgledy-piggledy approach to fruit distribution. You can pile it as high as you like, but be warned that it can get a bit messy when serving. This does not in any way affect the taste.

To make the pastry cream, put the milk and vanilla pod in a heavy saucepan and bring just to the boil. Remove from the heat, cover and leave to infuse for 15 minutes.

Put the egg yolks and sugar in a heatproof bowl and whisk well. Add the flour and mix well. Strain the milk into the yolk mixture and whisk until smooth. Return to the saucepan and continue cooking over low heat for 2 minutes, stirring constantly. It will thicken. Transfer to a shallow bowl to cool. (This can be prepared up to 1 day in advance if covered and refrigerated.)

Spread the pastry cream in an even layer in the cooled tart shell. Arrange the fruit on top. You can start with one kind, using almost all of it, and then go on to another, until you've used all the types. Then go back and fill in the holes with the remaining pieces.

Melt the jam and 2 tablespoons water in a small saucepan set over low heat. Strain to remove all the lumpy bits. Using a pastry brush, carefully but generously dab or brush the jam over the fruit to form a shiny glaze. Let cool. Refrigerate for 6–8 hours in advance, but return to almost room temperature to serve.

Variation
For a fresh strawberry tart, use 2–3 large punnets of washed and dried strawberries, halved and/or sliced depending on size. Glaze with redcurrant jelly instead of apricot jam – it shouldn't need straining.

Tarte au citron

**500 g/1 lb. 2 oz.
storebought shortcrust
pastry (thawed if frozen)**
**plain/all-purpose flour,
for dusting**
**icing/confectioners' sugar,
for dusting**

CUSTARD
8 eggs
**300 g/1½ cups caster/
granulated sugar**
**grated zest and freshly
squeezed juice of
4 lemons**
**freshly squeezed juice
of 2 limes**
**300 ml/1¼ cups double/
heavy cream**

*23-cm/9-in. loose-bottom,
round, fluted tart pan,
greased*
baking beans
kitchen blowtorch

SERVES 10

Lemon tart is a classic French pâtisserie delight. It has a sharp citrus flavour and makes a delicious treat served with fresh blueberries and a little cream.

On a flour-dusted surface, roll out the pastry thinly into a circle just larger than the size of your tart pan. Using the rolling pin to help lift it, carefully move the pastry into the pan and press it down so that it fits snugly. Trim away any excess pastry using a sharp knife, but leave some pastry hanging over the edge of the pan. This will be trimmed neatly after the tart is baked. Prick the base with a fork and chill in the refrigerator for 30 minutes.

Preheat the oven to 200°C (400°F) Gas 6.

Line the pastry with baking parchment, fill with baking beans and bake blind for about 15–20 minutes in the preheated oven, until the pastry is lightly golden brown. Remove the baking beans and parchment, and let cool. Turn the oven temperature down to 180°C (350°F) Gas 4.

Whisk together the eggs, sugar, lemon zest and juice, and lime juice in a bowl. Slowly pour in the cream, whisking all the time. Place in a heatproof bowl set over a pan of simmering water and heat until the mixture becomes just warm. This will take about 5 minutes.

Pour the custard into the pastry case. You may not need all of the filling, depending on the size of your pan. Bake for 30–40 minutes, until the top of the custard is lightly golden and has risen. Remove from the oven and let cool. The custard will sink back into the pastry case as it cools.

Use a sharp knife to trim away the excess pastry around the top of the pan so that the pastry is in line with the top of the tart pan. Dust with icing/confectioners' sugar to serve. This tart will keep for up to 3 days stored in the refrigerator.

Rhubarb tart

150 g/generous 1 cup plain/all-purpose flour
1 teaspoon baking powder
100 g/7 tablespoons butter, softened and diced
85 g/scant ½ cup caster/superfine sugar
1 egg yolk

FILLING
300 g/10½ oz. rhubarb, trimmed and roughly chopped
2 tablespoons dark brown soft sugar
50 g/3½ tablespoons butter, softened and diced
60 g/generous ¼ cup caster/superfine sugar
50 g/generous ½ cup rolled (porridge) oats

20-cm/8-in. loose-bottomed, fluted tart pan, greased

SERVES 6–8

The base for this tart is a lovely cross between pastry and biscuit. When you mix the dough, it will feel wet, but that is how it should be - just flour your hands before you press the dough into the tart pan.

Preheat the oven to 200°C (400°F) Gas 6.

Sift the flour and baking powder into a mixing bowl. Rub the butter into the flour mixture with your fingertips until it looks like breadcrumbs. Stir in the sugar and egg yolk and mix until a dough forms.

Transfer the dough to the tart pan and push and press it into the pan until the base and sides are evenly covered with a neat layer of dough.

To make the filling, put the rhubarb and brown sugar in a bowl and mix until the rhubarb is evenly coated, then transfer to the pastry case and spread roughly over the base of the tart.

In a separate bowl, mix the butter, caster sugar and oats together until you have a rough mixture like a crumble topping. Scatter roughly over the rhubarb filling.

Bake in the preheated oven for 30 minutes, or until the crumble topping and pastry are golden brown.

Summer berry lattice tart

7 g/¼ oz. instant/easy-
blend dried yeast

500 g/3½–3⅔ cups strong
white bread flour

250 ml/1 cup lukewarm
milk

85 g/generous ⅓ cup
caster/superfine sugar

½ teaspoon salt

1 egg, lightly beaten

75 g/¾ stick butter,
softened

icing/confectioners' sugar,
for dusting

whipped cream, to serve

FILLING

3 tablespoons cornflour/
cornstarch

3 tablespoons caster/
superfine sugar

500 g/1 lb. 2 oz.
blueberries or a mixture
of summer berries
(if using frozen berries,
defrost them in a sieve/
strainer in advance to
drain off the excess
liquid)

40 g/½ cup dried
breadcrumbs

*23 x 32-cm/9 x 13-in
roasting tray, lined with
baking parchment*

SERVES 6–8

This pretty, rustic tart is traditionally made with wild blueberries, which are smaller and less sweet than the cultivated ones. You can use any blueberries you like or even a mixture of summer berries, which add a little sharpness and contrast with the softness of the pastry.

Mix the yeast and flour together in a bowl.

Put the milk, sugar, salt and half the egg in a mixing bowl and whisk together. Tip the flour mixture into the bowl and mix, kneading with your hands when it gets firm. Finally, add the butter and knead it into the dough with your hands until thoroughly incorporated. Cover with a clean tea towel and leave to prove in a warm place for 30 minutes.

Preheat the oven to 200°C (400°F) Gas 6.

To make the filling, put the cornflour, sugar and berries in a separate bowl and mix until the berries are evenly coated.

Punch down the dough and roll out on a lightly floured surface, with a rolling pin, until it is 4 cm /1½ in. larger than the prepared roasting tray. (Reserve the pastry offcuts for the lattice topping.) Gently and loosely roll the pastry around the rolling pin and transfer it to the prepared roasting tray. Line the tray with the pastry – the pastry should line the base of the tray and go only slightly up the sides. Neatly cut off the excess pastry.

Sprinkle the breadcrumbs over the pastry case, then spread the berry mixture evenly over the top.

To make the lattice topping, gather up the offcuts of pastry and roll out on the floured work surface again. Cut into long strips and lay four strips diagonally across the top of the tart, trimming the strips to fit. Repeat with four strips in the opposite direction. Stick the ends of the strips to the edge of the tart with a dab of water. Brush the remaining beaten egg over the pastry to glaze.

Bake in the preheated oven for 30 minutes. Leave to cool slightly, then dust with icing sugar and serve warm with a dollop of whipped cream.

Blueberry tart with rye

100 g/7 tablespoons
  butter, softened
85 g/generous ⅓ cup
  caster/superfine sugar
1 egg, lightly beaten
100 g/¾ cup plain/
  all-purpose flour
60 g/scant ½ cup
  wholemeal rye flour
1 teaspoon baking powder

FILLING
100 g/3½ oz. crème
  fraîche
150 ml/⅔ cup soured
  cream
1 egg, lightly beaten
40 g/scant ¼ cup
  caster/superfine sugar
1 teaspoon pure vanilla
  extract
250 g/9 oz. blueberries

24-cm/9½-in. loose-
  bottomed, fluted tart
  pan, greased

SERVES 6–8

Another popular tart, but with a crème fraîche and soured cream topping. It's a simple and attractive option for the end of a casual summer meal with friends.

Preheat the oven to 200°C (400°F) Gas 6.

Put the butter and sugar in a mixing bowl and beat until well mixed. Gradually add the egg, mixing well. Tip in the flours and baking powder and mix again until a dough has formed.

Transfer the dough to the tart pan and press it into the pan until the base and sides are evenly covered with a neat layer of dough.

To make the filling, put the crème fraîche, soured cream, egg, sugar and vanilla extract in a mixing bowl and mix well. Pour into the pastry case, then scatter the blueberries into the tart.

Bake in the preheated oven for 25 minutes, or until the filling has set and the pastry is golden brown.

Apricot vanilla tart

500 g/1 lb. 2 oz. storebought shortcrust pastry (thawed if frozen)

plain/all-purpose flour, for dusting

ROASTED APRICOTS

16 apricots, halved and stoned/pitted

50 g/¼ cup caster/granulated sugar

freshly squeezed juice of 1 lemon

50 g/3½ tablespoons butter

FILLING

250 g/generous 1 cup mascarpone cheese

150 ml/⅔ cup crème fraîche

100 g/3½ oz. vanilla custard

½ teaspoon vanilla bean powder or 1 teaspoon pure vanilla extract

1 heaped tablespoon icing/confectioners' sugar, sifted

GLAZE

2 tablespoons apricot glaze or apricot jam/jelly

freshly squeezed juice of 1 lemon

23-cm/9-in. loose-bottom, round, fluted tart pan, greased

baking beans

SERVES 8

Unless they are really ripe, apricots can taste a little bland. However, when roasted with a little butter, sugar and lemon juice, they become the perfect topping for this sunny tart.

Preheat the oven to 180°C (350°F) Gas 4.

Place the apricots, cut-side down, in a roasting pan and sprinkle with the sugar and lemon juice. Add the butter and bake for 15–20 minutes, until the fruit is just soft. Remove from the oven and let cool. Increase the oven temperature to 200°C (400°F) Gas 6.

On a flour-dusted surface, roll out the pastry thinly into a circle just larger than the size of your tart pan. Using the rolling pin to help lift it, carefully move the pastry into the pan and press it down so that it fits snugly. Trim away any excess pastry using a sharp knife, but leave some pastry hanging over the edge of the pan. This will be trimmed neatly after the tart is baked. Prick the base with a fork and chill in the refrigerator for 30 minutes.

Line the pastry case with baking parchment, fill with baking beans and bake blind for about 20–25 minutes in the centre of the preheated oven, until the pastry is golden brown and crisp. When cool enough to handle, remove the baking beans and parchment. Trim the edge of the pastry with a sharp knife by running it along the top of the pan.

Blitz about one-third of the apricots and the cooking syrup to a purée in a food processor or blender and pass through a fine-mesh sieve/strainer so that the purée is smooth. In a bowl, whisk together the apricot purée, mascarpone cheese, crème fraîche, custard, vanilla and icing sugar until smooth. Spoon the mixture into the pastry case and spread out evenly using a spatula.

Place the remaining apricots on top of the cream filling, moving them carefully with a spatula so that they retain their shape.

In a saucepan, heat the apricot glaze and lemon juice until melted. If using apricot jam, you may need to strain the heated syrup to remove any apricot pieces. Leave to cool slightly, then brush over the top of the fruit with a pastry brush.

Chill in the refrigerator for at least 2 hours before serving. This tart will keep for up to 3 days stored in the refrigerator.

Green tea cream tart with strawberries

1 storebought pre-baked
sweet pastry tart shell

GREEN TEA PASTRY CREAM

4 teaspoons high-quality
green tea powder
(matcha powder)

250 ml/1 cup milk

60 g/generous ½ cup
caster/superfine sugar

2 egg yolks

½ teaspoon pure vanilla
extract

1 tablespoon cornflour/
cornstarch

35 g/2½ tablespoons
butter

TO DECORATE

2 punnets of ripe
strawberries, hulled
(leave stalks on the
prettiest ones and
reserve for decoration)

70 g/2½ oz. strawberry
jam/jelly

white chocolate, melted,
for drizzling

SERVES 8–10

This dessert should really only be made during strawberry season; out-of-season strawberries will be too bland to stand up to the strong taste of the green tea.

First, make the flavoured pastry cream. Put the tea powder, milk and half the sugar in a medium saucepan over a medium heat and stir with a wooden spoon. Bring to a simmering boil. As soon as it comes to a simmering boil, remove from the heat, cover and set aside.

Put the egg yolks and vanilla extract in a large, heatproof bowl. In a separate bowl, combine the remaining sugar and the cornflour and mix thoroughly. Add to the egg yolks and whisk thoroughly. While the milk mixture is still hot, whisk it into the egg mixture in the bowl. Strain the mixture back into the saucepan, set over medium–low heat and whisk continuously until it reaches a boil.

Strain the mixture again into a bowl and stir in the butter until melted and thoroughly combined. Lay a sheet of clingfilm/plastic wrap directly on the surface of the pastry cream, then let cool. Chill for 30 minutes before using.

Spoon the green tea pastry cream into the tart shell and level with a spatula. Scatter the strawberries over the top in a decorative fashion, as you wish.

To decorate, put the strawberry jam and 1 tablespoon water in a small saucepan and bring to a boil, so that the jam is thin and hot. Brush or pour the glaze all over the strawberries, especially the cut tops, to make a glaze.

Drizzle melted white chocolate all over the strawberries to decorate.

Cherry pie

500 g/1 lb. 2 oz.
  storebought puff pastry
  (thawed if frozen)
plain/all-purpose flour,
  for dusting
1 egg, beaten

CHERRY FILLING
400 g/2⅔ cups cherries,
  stoned/pitted and stalks
  removed
150 g/¾ cup caster/
  superfine sugar, plus
  extra for sprinkling
freshly squeezed juice
  of 1 lemon
15 g/1 tablespoon butter
1 tablespoon cornflour/
  cornstarch

23-cm/9-in. round pie dish,
  greased

SERVES 6–8

This cherry pie has a decorative lattice topping and is great to serve in the summer when cherries are ripe and plentiful. If you are short of time, you can replace the filling with a can of cherry pie filling instead, but add the freshly squeezed juice of a lemon to give it a little extra zing.

Begin by preparing the cherry filling, as this needs to cool before making the pie. Simmer the cherries with 80 ml/⅓ cup water, the sugar and the lemon juice in a saucepan, until the cherries are soft and the juice is syrupy. Add the butter and stir until melted. Mix the cornflour with one tablespoon of the cherry juice removed from the pan and then stir into the cherries and juice. Simmer for a few minutes, until the sauce has thickened. Set aside to cool.

Preheat the oven to 200°C (400°F) Gas 6.

On a flour-dusted surface, roll out one-half of the pastry into a circle just larger than the size of your pie dish. Using the rolling pin to help lift it, carefully move the pastry into the dish and press it down so that it fits snugly. Brush the inside of the pastry with some of the beaten egg using a pastry brush, brushing all the way to the edges as the lattice strips need to stick to this edge.

Spoon the cooled cherry filling into the centre of the pastry case. Roll out the remaining pastry into a square just larger than your pie dish, and cut into thin strips. Weave the strips together into a lattice pattern, then transfer the lattice to the pie and press the strips down to join them to the edge of the bottom layer of pastry. Trim any excess pastry with a sharp knife. Brush the top of the pastry with a little more beaten egg and sprinkle with sugar.

Bake in the preheated oven for 25–30 minutes, until the pastry has risen and is golden brown. Serve warm or cold with cream. The pie is best eaten on the day it is made, although can be stored in an airtight container and eaten the following day.

Rhubarb meringue pie

Rhubarb is the quintessential summer fruit with the sharpness working perfectly with the decadent meringue topping.

100 g/1 stick unsalted butter, softened at room temperature
65 g/⅓ cup caster/superfine sugar
2 eggs, separated
90 g/⅔ cup plain/all-purpose flour
1 teaspoon baking powder
50 ml/scant ¼ cup milk

FILLING
3–4 sticks of rhubarb, trimmed and roughly chopped
1 teaspoon ground cinnamon
65 g/⅓ cup caster/superfine sugar
1 teaspoon pure vanilla extract
50 g/generous ½ cup flaked/sliced almonds

24-cm/9½-in. loose-bottomed, fluted tart pan, greased

SERVES 6–8

Preheat the oven to 180°C (350°F) Gas 4.

Cream the butter and sugar until pale and fluffy. Add the egg yolks one by one, mixing well. Mix the flour and baking powder together, then add half to the butter mixture, mixing well.

Add half the milk and mix well. Finally, add the remaining flour mixture, mix, then add the remaining milk and mix well. Transfer the dough to the tart pan and push and press it until the base and sides are evenly covered with a layer of dough.

To make the filling, mix the rhubarb, cinnamon and 2 teaspoons of the sugar together, then spread roughly over the tart. Whisk the egg whites until they hold soft peaks, then gradually add the remaining sugar, whisking until firm. Fold in the vanilla extract.

Spoon on top of the pie, making peaks as you go, and scatter the almonds over the top. Bake in the preheated oven for 35–40 minutes.

Blueberry pie

500 g/1 lb. 2 oz.
   storebought puff pastry
   (thawed if frozen)
plain/all-purpose flour,
   for dusting
1 egg, beaten

BLUEBERRY FILLING
600 g/5 cups blueberries
freshly squeezed juice and
   grated zest of 2 lemons
100 g/½ cup caster/
   superfine sugar, plus
   extra for sprinkling
2 tablespoons cornflour/
   cornstarch, sifted

23-cm/9-in. round pie dish,
   greased

SERVES 6–8

The aroma of this pie when you remove it from the oven is heavenly, and it takes a lot of willpower to resist digging in immediately with a spoon. You can serve it warm with cream or custard, but it is also nice served cold on its own.

Preheat the oven to 200°C (400°F) Gas 6.

On a flour-dusted surface, roll out the pastry thinly using a rolling pin until it is a circle about 6 cm/2½ in. larger than the size of your pie dish. Using the rolling pin to help lift it, carefully move the pastry into the dish and press it down so that it fits snugly in the dish with some of the pastry hanging over the top edge. Brush the inside of the pastry case with some of the beaten egg using a pastry brush. This will help prevent the pastry becoming soggy.

Place the blueberries, lemon juice and zest, sugar and cornflour in a bowl. Stir well so that everything is mixed together.

Spoon the blueberry mixture into the pie dish, piling it high in the centre. Lift the edges of the pastry up over the blueberries and crimp together with your fingers to make a decorative pattern. The centre of the pie should remain open so that you can see the blueberries.

Brush the top of the pastry with the remaining beaten egg and sprinkle with sugar.

Bake the pie in the preheated oven for 40–50 minutes, until the pastry is crisp and golden brown.

Remove from the oven and leave to cool slightly, if serving warm, to allow the sauce to thicken. Alternatively, leave to cool completely and serve cold. This pie is best eaten on the day it is made, although can be stored in an airtight container and eaten the following day if you wish.

Lattice-topped cherry pie

CREAM CHEESE PASTRY
300 g/2⅓ cups plain/ all-purpose flour
2 tablespoons icing/ confectioners' sugar
a large pinch of salt
175 g/1½ sticks butter, chilled and diced
175 g/¾ cup full-fat cream cheese
4–6 tablespoons milk, chilled, plus extra to glaze

CHERRY FILLING
3 x 350-g/12-oz. packs frozen pitted Morello cherries (or 1 kg/2¼ lbs., drained weight, canned Morello cherries)
200 g/1 cup caster/ superfine sugar, plus extra for sprinkling
½ teaspoon ground cinnamon or a good pinch of allspice
freshly squeezed juice of 1 lemon
5 tablespoons cornflour/ cornstarch

23-cm/9-in. metal or enamel pie plate
baking sheet lined with baking parchment

SERVES 6

A favourite summer pie – it is so simple and is best made with luscious Morello cherries if you can get hold of them.

For the pastry, sift the flour into a large mixing bowl with the icing/ confectioners' sugar and salt. Rub in the butter and cream cheese until the mixture resembles coarse breadcrumbs. Add enough of the milk to mix to a soft dough. Gather up the dough to form a ball and knead very briefly until smooth. Divide into 2 pieces, then wrap and chill both portions in the refrigerator for at least 1 hour.

For the filling, mix the cherries with all the remaining ingredients and leave to stand for 20 minutes, then stir once more.

Preheat the oven to 220°C (425°F) Gas 7.

On a lightly floured surface, roll out half the pastry and use it to line the pie plate. Roll out the second half of the dough to a rectangle and cut into wide strips long enough to drape over the pie. Put the strips onto the prepared baking sheet and chill until needed.

Spoon the cherries into the lined pie plate, mounding them up in the centre. Brush the edges of the pastry with water, then lay the pastry strips on top, weaving them to form a lattice. Trim the edges, then crimp to seal. Brush the top with milk and sprinkle with sugar.

Set the pie on a baking sheet to catch any juices and bake in the preheated oven for 20 minutes to set the pastry. Reduce the oven temperature to 180°C (350°F) Gas 4 and bake for a further 30–40 minutes until the thickened cherry juices bubble up through the lattice. Cover the top loosely with kitchen foil if the pastry looks as if it is browning too quickly. Serve warm or cold.

Tip
This pie is very juicy – you may want to keep some juices back and boil separately to thicken them.

Pile-high peach pie

500 g/1 lb. 2 oz.
   storebought shortcrust
   pastry (thawed if frozen)
plain/all-purpose flour,
   for dusting
1 egg, beaten

PEACH FILLING
8 ripe peaches, stoned/
   pitted
2 tablespoons cornflour/
   cornstarch, sifted
70 g/⅓ cup caster/
   granulated sugar, plus
   extra for sprinkling
½ teaspoon vanilla salt
   (or ½ teaspoon salt plus
   ½ teaspoon pure vanilla
   extract)

23-cm/9-in. round pie dish,
   greased

SERVES 6–8

Fruit pies should always be bursting with filling and this pie is a perfect example. It is best made in the summer with ripe peaches when they are in season. The pretty heart shapes cut into the crust create an attractive finish.

Preheat the oven to 200°C (400°F) Gas 6.

On a flour-dusted surface, roll out one-half of the pastry into a circle just larger than the size of your pie dish. Using the rolling pin to help lift it, carefully move the pastry into the dish and press it down so that it fits snugly. Brush the inside of the pastry with some of the beaten egg using a pastry brush. This will help prevent the pastry becoming soggy.

Cut the peaches into thick slices and place in a bowl with the cornflour, sugar and salt. Toss gently with your hands so that the peaches are coated evenly. Pile the peaches into the pie case.

Roll the remaining pastry out into a circle slightly larger than the size of the dish. Cut out some heart shapes from the centre of the pastry, and reserve the pastry hearts. Brush the edges of the bottom pastry layer with a little beaten egg, then place the second pastry circle on top, so that you can see the filling through the heart-shaped holes. Crimp the edges of the pastry together with your fingertips or with the prongs of a fork, trimming away excess pastry. Brush the top of the pastry with the remaining egg and stick the pastry hearts decoratively on the top, brushing the hearts with a little more beaten egg. Sprinkle with sugar.

Bake in the preheated oven for 30–40 minutes, until the pastry is golden brown. This pie is best eaten on the day it is made, although it can be stored in the refrigerator and eaten the following day if you wish.

FRUITY FORK
DESSERTS

Rhubarb & custard slice

150 g/5¼ oz. storebought puff pastry

300 g/10½ oz. rhubarb

vegetable oil, to coat

50 g/¼ cup Demerara/raw sugar

200 ml/generous ¾ cup milk

100 ml/scant ½ cup double/heavy cream

2 eggs

2 egg yolks

50 g/⅓ cup plain/all-purpose flour

1 teaspoon pure vanilla extract

100 g/½ cup caster/superfine sugar

30 x 20-cm/12 x 8-in. brownie pan, lightly oiled and lined with baking parchment

MAKES 10

This slice is a take on a classic custard slice, which brings back childhood memories for so many of us, especially when it's paired with the magical combination of rhubarb and custard. Use storebought pastry; homemade puff pastry will shrink too much, and is too buttery and soft for this recipe.

Preheat the oven to 180°C (350°F) Gas 4.

Roll out the pastry to a thickness of about 3 mm/⅛ in. and trim it to fit the base of the brownie pan. Use a fork to prick holes all over the base; this will stop the pastry rising too much. Bake in the preheated oven for 10–12 minutes until the top is golden and the pastry is cooked through. Don't worry too much if your pastry shrinks a little as you can trim the edges later. Remove from the oven and leave to cool. Leave the oven on.

Trim and cut the rhubarb into evenly-sized pieces, about 2 cm/¾ in. in length. Toss them with a little vegetable oil and then the Demerara sugar. Spread the rhubarb out on the lined baking sheet. Bake in the oven for 10–12 minutes, until they are just softened and cooked through.

In a heavy-bottomed saucepan, heat the milk and cream over low heat, gently stirring, until just simmering, then take immediately off the heat. In a mixing bowl, whisk together the eggs, egg yolks, flour, vanilla and caster sugar to form a paste. Pour the hot milk and cream mixture into the mixing bowl, whisking constantly to combine into a thin custard.

Now return the custard to the saucepan and, carefully, over low heat so as not to catch or burn it, whisk the custard over the heat until it is thickened and holding soft peaks.

Pour the thick custard over the pastry base and smooth it to make level. Carefully, place the rhubarb pieces on top of the custard; they should be half-submerged in the custard.

Place the brownie pan in the refrigerator for at least an hour before carefully removing and cutting the slice into 10 with a bread knife.

Strawberry layer cake with Chantilly cream

340 g/3 sticks butter, softened

340 g/1¾ cups caster/granulated sugar

6 eggs

340 g/2½ cups self-raising/self-rising flour, sifted

3 teaspoons baking powder

3 tablespoons buttermilk or sour cream

1 teaspoon vanilla bean powder or 2 teaspoons pure vanilla extract

600 g/1 lb. 5 oz. strawberries

5 tablespoons strawberry jam/jelly

icing/confectioners' sugar, for dusting

a few strawberry leaves, for decoration

CHANTILLY CREAM

600 ml/2½ cups double/heavy cream

1 teaspoon vanilla bean powder or seeds of 1 vanilla pod/bean

2 tablespoons icing/confectioners' sugar, sifted

20-cm/8-in. and 25-cm/10-in. square loose-bottom cake pans, greased and lined with baking parchment

SERVES 18

This is a perfect summertime cake with cream and fresh berries and perfectly scented with vanilla.

Preheat the oven to 180°C (350°F) Gas 4.

Use an electric whisk to mix the butter and sugar in a bowl until light and creamy. Add the eggs and whisk again. Fold in the flour, baking powder and buttermilk or sour cream using a spatula, until incorporated.

Fold the vanilla into the cake batter and spoon the mixture into the prepared cake pans, dividing the mixture approximately two-thirds into the larger pan and the remaining one-third into the smaller pan, so that the depth of the cakes is equal.

Bake in the preheated oven for 30–40 minutes, until the cakes are golden brown and spring back to the touch and a knife inserted into the centre of each cake comes out clean. The smaller cake will take less time to cook than the larger one, so check it regularly towards the end of the cooking time. Leave the cakes to cool in the pans for a few minutes, then turn out onto a wire rack to cool completely.

For the Chantilly cream, put the cream, vanilla and icing sugar in a large bowl and whisk to stiff peaks. Set aside one or two of the whole strawberries for decoration, then hull and slice the remaining fruit.

Cut each cake in half horizontally using a large serrated knife. Place the bottom half of the larger cake on a serving plate and spread cream across the surface. Cover the cream with some of the strawberry slices and 3 tablespoons of the jam. Top with the second large cake half and dust the top with icing sugar. Spoon a tablespoonful of the jam in the centre and spread out a little, keeping it in the centre of the cake so that it will all be covered by the smaller cake – this will hold the smaller cake in place. Place the bottom of the smaller cake on top of the jam and repeat the above steps with the cream and the remaining strawberries and jam. Place the second half of the small cake on top and dust with icing sugar. Decorate with the reserved whole strawberries and a few strawberry leaves. The leaves should be removed before you cut the cake.

Serve straight away or store in the refrigerator until you are ready to serve. As the cake contains cream, it is best eaten on the day it is made.

Key lime 'pie'

PIE CRUST
250 g/9 oz. custard creams/vanilla sandwich cookies or digestive biscuits/graham crackers
100 g/7 tablespoons butter, melted

LIME FILLING
6 limes
300 ml/1¼ cups double/heavy cream
400-g/14-oz. can sweetened condensed milk

TO DECORATE
200 ml/scant 1 cup double/heavy cream
chocolate sprinkles
freshly grated lime zest

23-cm/9-in. loose-bottom, round, fluted tart pan, greased

SERVES 10

Not a pie in the traditional sense, but this biscuit-based dessert made with fresh and zingy limes makes a great dessert as it can be prepared ahead of time. I like to use custard creams/vanilla sandwich cookies for the base, but you can replace them with digestives/graham crackers, if you prefer.

Preheat the oven to 180°C (350°F) Gas 4.

Blitz the cookies to fine crumbs in a food processor or blender, or place in a clean plastic bag and bash with a rolling pin. Stir in the melted butter and then press into the base and the sides of the prepared tart pan firmly using the back of a spoon. Wrap the base and sides of the pan in foil to prevent butter from leaking out, then bake the cookie crust in the oven for 5–8 minutes, then allow to cool completely.

Finely grate the zest of 2 of the limes into a mixing bowl. Add the cream, condensed milk, and the juice of all 6 limes. (Zest the remaining limes before juicing, and reserve for the decoration.) Whisk until smooth. Spoon the mixture into the pie crust and chill in the refrigerator for at least 3 hours, until set, or overnight.

To decorate, place the cream in a bowl and whip to stiff peaks with a whisk. Spoon the whipped cream on top of the pie, and decorate with chocolate sprinkles and the reserved freshly grated lime zest. This pie will keep in the refrigerator for 2 days.

Glazed mango mousse pie

PIE CRUST
250 g/9 oz. ginger biscuits/cookies
150 g/1 stick plus 2 tablespoons butter, melted

MANGO MOUSSE
1 large ripe mango
70 g/5⅔ tablespoons caster/superfine sugar
freshly squeezed juice of 1 lemon
12 g/4 teaspoons powdered gelatine
300 ml/1¼ cups double/ heavy cream

TO DECORATE
1 ripe mango
about 20 strawberries

GLAZE
2 sheets of leaf gelatine
freshly squeezed juice of 2 lemons
30 g/2½ tablespoons caster/superfine sugar
1 packet glaze topping/ fixing gel, such as Dr Oetker's (optional)

35 x 10-cm/14 x 4-in. loose-bottom, rectangular, fluted tart pan, greased

SERVES 8

Tropical mangoes are juicy and tangy, and they make the perfect filling for this sunshine pie. Topped with thin slices of mango and strawberries, this pie looks as pretty as a picture. Make your own glaze or use a storebought one to save time.

Blitz the biscuits/cookies to fine crumbs in a food processor or blender, or place in a clean plastic bag and bash with a rolling pin. Add the melted butter and sugar, and mix again so that all the crumbs are coated in butter. Using the back of a spoon, press the crumb mixture into the prepared pan so that the sides have a thick layer of crumbs on and the base is completely covered, with no gaps.

For the mousse, peel the mango and chop the flesh away from the stone/pit. Place the flesh in a blender with the sugar and lemon juice, and blitz to a smooth purée. Dissolve the gelatine in 1 tablespoon of warm water and then add to the mango mixture. Whip the cream to stiff peaks and then fold through the mango purée, whisking gently so that it is all incorporated. Pour the mousse into the pie crust and chill in the refrigerator for at least 3 hours.

When the mousse is set, finely slice the mango and strawberries for decoration, and arrange in patterns on top of the mango mousse.

If you are making your own glaze, soak the gelatine leaves in cold water. Heat the lemon juice with 250 ml/1 cup water and the sugar, until the sugar has dissolved and the mixture is warm but not boiling (having the liquid too hot will affect the setting properties of the gelatine). Stir in the gelatine until dissolved, then strain through a sieve/strainer. Leave until just cool. Alternatively, prepare the glaze topping/fixing gel according to the packet instructions. Pour the glaze over the fruit and leave to set in the fridge overnight.

This pie will keep for up to 2 days in the refrigerator.

Lemon, cardamom & raspberry torte

125 g/1 stick plus 1 tablespoon butter, plus extra for greasing

200 g/1 cup golden caster/superfine sugar

10 cardamom pods, seeds crushed

finely grated zest of 1 unwaxed lemon

2 teaspoons pure vanilla extract

3 large/US extra-large eggs

200 g/1 cup raspberries or blueberries

250 g/1½ cups ground almonds

a pinch of salt

1 teaspoon baking powder (gluten-free)

LEMON DRIZZLE ICING

200 g/1½ cups icing/confectioners' sugar

finely grated zest and freshly squeezed juice of 1 small lemon

handful of toasted hazelnuts, finely chopped

23-cm/9-in. springform cake pan, greased and lined

SERVES 6–8

A divine summery flourless cake, which works just as well with blueberries as it does with raspberries.

Preheat the oven to 170°C (325°F) Gas 3.

Cream together the butter, sugar, cardamom seeds, lemon zest and vanilla extract until pale and fluffy. Add the eggs one at a time and beat between each addition.

Fold in the fruit, ground almonds, salt and baking powder. Fill the cake pan with the mixture and bake in the preheated oven for 45 minutes until golden, and a skewer inserted into the centre comes out cleanly. Cool on a wire rack and then unmould.

To make the lemon drizzle icing, mix the lemon zest and juice with the icing sugar. Pour over the cooled cake and sprinkle with toasted hazelnuts.

Peach melba meringue layer

225 g/2 sticks butter, softened

225 g/generous 1 cup caster/superfine sugar

4 eggs

225 g/1¾ cups self-raising/self-rising flour, sifted

2 teaspoons baking powder

2 tablespoons buttermilk or sour cream

1 teaspoon vanilla bean paste or pure vanilla extract

icing/confectioners' sugar, for dusting

MERINGUE

4 egg whites

225g/1 cup plus 1 tablespoon caster/superfine sugar

PEACH FILLING

8 peaches

500 ml/2 cups double/heavy cream, whipped

400 g/14 oz. raspberries

2 x 20-cm/8-in. round cake pans, greased and lined with baking parchment

2 baking sheets, lined with baking parchment

SERVES 12

The retro dessert peach melba is the inspiration for this decadent layer cake. With crisp meringue, poached peaches, raspberries and cream, it is ideal for any summer special occasion.

Preheat the oven to 140°C (275°F) Gas 1.

To prepare the meringue, whisk the egg whites to stiff peaks using an electric hand mixer. Add the sugar, a spoonful at a time, whisking after each spoonful until you have a thick glossy meringue that holds a peak when you lift the beaters.

On the prepared baking sheets, make two 20-cm/8-in. circles of meringue, swirling the tops into decorative peaks. Bake in the preheated oven for 1½ hours, until the meringues are crisp, then leave to cool on the baking sheet. Turn the oven up to 180°C (350°F) Gas 4.

To make the cake mix, use an electric whisk to mix the butter and sugar in a bowl until light and creamy. Add the eggs and whisk again. Fold in the flour, baking powder and buttermilk or sour cream using a spatula, until incorporated. Fold the vanilla into the cake batter and divide the mixture equally between the prepared cake pans. Bake for about 20–30 minutes, until the cakes are golden brown and spring back to the touch and a knife inserted into the centre of each cake comes out clean. Leave to cool in the pans for a few minutes, then turn out onto a wire rack to cool completely.

Put the peaches in a bowl and pour over boiling water to cover them. Leave for a few minutes, then drain. When the peaches are just cool enough to handle, peel away their skins, which will have been loosened by the hot water. Remove the stones/pits and cut the flesh into slices.

To assemble, place one of the cakes on a serving plate and dust with icing sugar. Top with one-third of the whipped cream and cover with half of the peach slices. Place one of the meringues on top and cover that with one-third of the cream and the raspberries. Next place the second sponge on top and dust with icing sugar. Cover with the remaining cream and peaches. To finish, place the second meringue on top and dust with a little more icing sugar.

Serve straight away or store in the refrigerator until you are ready to serve. As the cake contains fresh cream, it is best eaten on the day it is made, although it will keep for up to 2 days in the refrigerator.

Pina colada dream

PIE CRUST
300 g/10½ oz. coconut biscuits/cookies

120 g/1 stick butter, melted

FILLING
6 egg yolks

80 g/6½ tablespoons caster/superfine sugar

4 tablespoons coconut rum

250 ml/generous 1 cup double/heavy cream

150 ml/⅔ cup coconut milk

1 tablespoon melted butter

½ teaspoon vanilla bean powder or 1 teaspoon pure vanilla extract

TOPPING
50 g/¾ cup long, shredded, sweetened coconut

1 small pineapple

4 tablespoons coconut rum

300 ml/1¼ cups double/heavy cream

23-cm/9-in. loose-bottom, round, fluted tart pan, greased

SERVES 10

This sun-drenched dessert is inspired by holidays in Jamaica. Packed with exotic flavours, this is a perfect summer party pie.

Blitz the biscuits/cookies to fine crumbs in a food processor or blender, or place in a clean plastic bag and bash with a rolling pin. Stir in the melted butter, ensuring that all the crumbs are coated. Press the crumbs into the base and sides of the pan.

Preheat the oven to 150°C (300°F) Gas 2.

For the filling, whisk together the egg yolks and sugar until light and creamy. Slowly pour in the rum, cream, coconut milk, melted butter and vanilla, and whisk everything together.

Wrap the base and sides of the pan in foil and place on a baking sheet to catch any butter that might be released during baking. Pour the mixture into the pie crust. Transfer carefully to the oven.

Bake for 1½ hours, until the top of the custard is very lightly golden brown and set with a slight wobble still in the centre. Let cool.

For the topping, toast the coconut in a dry frying pan/skillet over gentle heat, until it is lightly golden brown, stirring all the time to ensure that it does not burn. Let cool.

Peel and core the pineapple and cut into small chunks. Place in a bowl and pour over the rum. Leave to soak.

Place the pie on a serving plate. Whip the cream to stiff peaks using a mixer or whisk. Spoon the cream over the coconut custard. Drain the pineapple and place on top of the cream. Sprinkle over the toasted coconut. Serve immediately, or store for up to 2 days in the refrigerator.

Blueberry & lemon drizzle cakes

225 g/2 sticks butter, softened

225 g/generous 1 cup caster/superfine sugar

4 eggs

225 g/1¾ cups self-raising/self-rising flour, sifted

2 teaspoons baking powder

2 tablespoons buttermilk or sour cream

grated zest of 2 lemons

200 ml/¾ cup double/heavy cream, whipped

4 tablespoons lemon curd

200 g/1½ cups blueberries

ICING

170 g/1¼ cups fondant icing/confectioners' sugar, sifted

freshly squeezed juice of 2 lemons

8 x 6.5-cm/2½-in. cake rings, greased and placed on a greased baking sheet

piping/pastry bag fitted with large round nozzle/tip (optional)

piping/pastry bag fitted with star nozzle/tip

MAKES 8

Tangy blueberries and zesty lemon are the perfect combination in these little cakes. Filled with whipped cream and lemon curd, these are great to serve for a summer tea party in the garden.

Preheat the oven to 180°C (350°F) Gas 4.

Use an electric whisk to mix the butter and sugar in a bowl until light and creamy. Add the eggs and whisk again. Fold in the flour, baking powder and buttermilk or sour cream using a spatula, until incorporated. Fold the lemon zest into the cake batter and divide the mixture equally between the prepared cake rings. You can do this either by spooning the batter in, or by putting the batter in a piping/pastry bag and piping it in neatly.

Bake in the oven for 20–30 minutes, until the cakes are golden brown and spring back to the touch. Leave the cakes to cool in the rings for a few minutes, then remove by sliding a sharp knife around the inside of each ring. Transfer the cakes to a wire rack and leave to cool completely.

Cut each cake in half and pipe a swirl of the whipped cream onto each bottom cake half using the piping/pastry bag with the star nozzle/tip. Top with a little lemon curd and a few blueberries, then place the top cake half on.

For the icing, mix together the fondant icing sugar and lemon juice (add the lemon juice gradually as you may not need it all), until you have a smooth, thick icing. Spoon the icing over the tops of the cakes, drizzling a few drops over the sides, and leave to set for a few minutes. Decorate with a few blueberries and leave the icing to set.

Store in the refrigerator until you are ready to serve. As these cakes contain fresh cream, they are best eaten on the day they are made, although they will keep for up to 2 days in the refrigerator, if necessary.

Lemon & raspberry roulade

150 ml/²⁄₃ cup milk

40 g/generous ¼ cup self-raising/self-rising flour, sifted

5 eggs, separated

150 g/¾ cup caster/superfine sugar

grated zest of 2 lemons

icing/confectioners' sugar, for dusting

FILLING

400 ml/1¾ cups double/heavy cream

4 tablespoons storebought custard/custard sauce

400 g/3½ cups raspberries

DECORATION

50 g/2 oz. white chocolate, melted

38 x 28-cm/15 x 11-in. Swiss roll/jelly roll pan, greased and lined with baking parchment

baking sheet, lined with a silicone mat or baking parchment

SERVES 6–8

Roulades are beautifully light and airy cakes, and make great dinner party desserts. Topped with just a dusting of powdered sugar and some white chocolate-dipped raspberries, this fresh and fruity cake is simply elegant and tastes delicious.

Preheat the oven to 200°C (400°F) Gas 6.

Heat the milk and flour together in a saucepan over low heat and whisk to a smooth paste.

In a mixing bowl, whisk the egg yolks and sugar together until thick and creamy and voluminous. Beat in the flour mixture and the grated lemon zest.

In a separate mixing bowl, whisk the egg whites to stiff peaks. Adding one-third at a time, fold the egg whites into the cake batter. Pour the mixture into the prepared pan and spread out evenly. Take care to handle the mixture gently so that you do not knock all the air out of it. Bake in the preheated oven for 8–12 minutes, until the sponge springs back to the touch and is golden brown.

Lay a sheet of non-stick baking parchment, larger than the size of the pan, on a flat surface. Dust with icing sugar. Remove the roulade from the oven and turn out onto the dusted parchment. Remove the lining paper, then roll the sponge up using the dusted parchment, so that the paper is inside the roll, and let cool.

When you are ready to serve, whip the cream to stiff peaks. Unroll the roulade. Using a spatula, spread a layer of whipped cream, followed by a layer of custard, onto the sponge. Sprinkle most of the raspberries evenly on top, reserving about 10 for decoration. Roll up the roulade, place it on a serving plate and dust with a little extra icing sugar.

Place the melted white chocolate in a small bowl and dip the reserved raspberries in to half-coat in the chocolate. Drizzle a little of the melted white chocolate along the top of the roulade to help the raspberries stick, then arrange the raspberries on the top. Serve straight away.

Gooseberry pavlova

MERINGUE LAYER

6 egg whites

**350 g/1¾ cups caster/
superfine sugar**

**1 teaspoon vanilla sugar
or the seeds from
1 vanilla pod/bean**

**2 teaspoons cornflour/
cornstarch**

a few drops of vinegar

GOOSEBERRY COMPOTE

**300 g/10½ oz.
gooseberries, topped
and tailed, plus extra
to garnish**

**2–3 tablespoons caster/
superfine sugar
(or more if needed)**

PASTRY CREAM

1 egg yolk

1 egg

**30 g/generous ¼ cup
cornflour/cornstarch**

**80 g/generous ⅓ cup
caster/granulated sugar**

¼ teaspoon salt

**500 ml/2 cups full-fat/
whole milk**

**seeds from 1 vanilla
pod/bean**

**25 g/1¾ tablespoons
butter**

**300 ml/1¼ cups whipping/
heavy cream**

*baking sheet, lined
with baking parchment*

SERVES 4–5

Gooseberries are often the forgotten summer fruit as their season is so short but the wonderfully tart berries with sweet meringue make a perfect summer dessert.

Preheat the oven to 120°C (250°F) Gas ½.

To make the meringue, whip the egg whites in the very clean bowl of a stand mixer or with a hand-held electric whisk until soft peaks form. Start to slowly add the sugar mixed with the vanilla, bit by bit. Continue whisking at high speed for around 4–5 minutes until the meringue is stiff and glossy. If you can no longer feel the sugar grains it is a good indication. Fold in the cornflour/cornstarch and vinegar.

Pile the meringue onto the prepared baking sheet in a loose rectangle shape. Bake in the warm oven for around 1½ hours or until crisp on the outside. Turn off the oven but leave the meringue inside to cool for a few hours if you can, with the door propped open with a wooden spoon.

Place the gooseberries in a saucepan with the sugar and a dash of water. Bring to the boil and cook for 3 minutes until the berries are soft. Mash lightly with a fork and taste – they might need more sugar. Gooseberries are delightful because they are sour, so don't add too much. Set the compote aside to cool, then refrigerate until needed.

For the pastry cream, whisk together the egg yolk and egg, cornflour, sugar and salt until well combined and set aside. Heat the milk and vanilla seeds until just boiling in a saucepan. Slowly pour one third of the milk into the egg and cornflour mixture, while whisking vigorously to incorporate but not scramble the eggs. Pour the egg mixture back into the saucepan with the rest of the milk. Whisk continuously and bring to the boil again for around 30 seconds until thickened. Remove from the heat and stir in the butter until melted. Pour into a bowl and leave to cool with a layer of baking parchment on top to prevent a skin from forming. Refrigerate, ideally for a few hours, before using.

When you are ready to assemble, whip the cream and fold together with the pastry cream. Place the meringue on a serving plate and pile over the whipped cream mixture. Top with the gooseberry compote and extra fresh gooseberries to garnish.

Lime Charlotte cake

115 g/1 stick butter, softened

115 g/generous ½ cup caster/superfine sugar

2 eggs

115 g/generous ¾ cup self-raising/self-rising flour, sifted

1 teaspoon baking powder

1 tablespoon buttermilk or sour cream

grated zest of 2 limes

200 g/7 oz. sponge finger biscuits/ladyfinger cookies

300 g/10½ oz. strawberries

icing/confectioners' sugar, for dusting

FILLING

freshly squeezed juice of 3 limes

grated zest of 1 lime

300 g/1⅓ cups cream cheese

200 g/scant 1 cup sweetened condensed milk

16-cm/6½-in. loose-bottom deep cake pan, greased and lined with baking parchment

pretty ribbon

SERVES 8

A traditional Charlotte makes such a pretty centrepiece dessert, tied with ribbons and topped with glistening berries. This lime sponge is topped with a tangy lime mousse, piled high with ripe and juicy berries.

Preheat the oven to 180°C (350°F) Gas 4.

Use an electric whisk to mix the butter and sugar in a bowl until light and creamy. Add the eggs and whisk again. Fold in the flour, baking powder and buttermilk or sour cream using a spatula, until incorporated. Fold the lime zest into the cake batter and spoon into the prepared cake pan. Bake in the preheated oven for 20–30 minutes, until the cake is golden brown and springs back to the touch and a knife inserted into the centre of the cake comes out clean. Let cool in the pan.

For the filling, put the lime juice and zest, cream cheese and condensed milk in a mixing bowl and whisk together until thick and creamy. Spoon the mousse on top of the cooled cake and chill in the refrigerator for at least 3 hours, or preferably overnight, until the mousse has set.

When you are ready to serve, slide a knife around the edge of the pan and remove the sides. Remove the pan base and lining paper and place the cake on a serving plate. Carefully press the sponge fingers into the sides of the cake. They should hold in place as they will stick to the mousse. Once you have placed the fingers in a ring around the cake, tie the ribbon around the cake to hold them firmly in place.

Remove most of the stalks of the strawberries, but leave a few in place for a pretty red and green contrast. Place the strawberries on top of the Charlotte, arranging the ones with stalks at the top. Dust with icing sugar and serve.

This cake will keep for up to 3 days stored in the refrigerator, but should only be assembled just before serving as the sponge fingers will become soft over time.

Raspberry chiffon layer cake

225 g/1¾ cups self-raising/
 self-rising flour
275 g/generous 1¼ cups
 caster/superfine sugar
1 teaspoon baking powder
6 UK large/US extra-large
 eggs, separated
freshly squeezed juice of
 3 lemons and grated zest
 of 1 lemon
½ teaspoon vanilla bean
 powder or pure vanilla
 extract
150 ml/⅔ cup vegetable
 oil
1 teaspoon cream of tartar

FILLING
400 ml/scant 1¾ cups
 double/heavy cream
300 g/10½ oz. raspberries
4 tablespoons lemon curd
 or lemon cheese
icing/confectioners' sugar,
 for dusting

25-cm/10-in. Angel cake
 pan or other ring cake
 pan, well-greased

SERVES 8–10

This light and airy cake has luscious layers of chiffon sponge, lemon curd, whipped cream and raspberries – it makes a perfect summer treat. The art of a beautiful chiffon cake is adding in as much air as possible using whipped egg whites and raising agents. This sponge is made using oil, so is a great dairy-free cake if you layer with just fruit and jam/jelly, rather than the curd and cream.

Preheat the oven to 180°C (350°F) Gas 4.

Sift the flour into a large mixing bowl. Add 225 g/generous 1 cup of the caster sugar and the baking powder and stir in so that everything is well mixed. Add the egg yolks, lemon juice and zest, vanilla and oil. Mix everything together well until the mixture is light and creamy.

In a separate bowl, whisk the egg whites to stiff peaks. Whisk in the cream of tartar and then add the remaining 50 g/¼ cup caster sugar, a spoonful at a time, whisking all the time to create a glossy meringue. Spoon one-third of the meringue into the flour mixture and fold in to loosen the batter. Add another third and fold in very gently. Add the remaining third and fold in. Pour the mixture into the prepared cake pan and bake for 35–40 minutes until the cake is golden brown and feels firm to touch. Remove from the oven and slide a knife around the edge and centre of the cake and leave to cool in the pan.

To assemble the cake, using a sharp bread knife, slice the cake into thirds horizontally so that you have three rings of cake. Place the bottom ring on your serving plate. To make the filling, whip the cream to stiff peaks using an electric mixer or whisk, and spoon half of the cream over the bottom cake. Top with half of the raspberries and drizzle with some of the lemon curd. Place a second ring of cake on top and repeat with the raspberries and lemon curd. Finally place the third cake on top and dust with icing sugar.

This cake is best eaten on the day it is made but will store for up to 2 days in an airtight container in the refrigerator.

PASTRY KNOW-HOW

Hints & tips

For perfect results every time, follow these simple and effective tips and hints for rolling, filling and baking pastry to perfection.

ROLLING THE PASTRY
• Pastry is easier to roll out if shaped into a ball, then flattened to a thick disk before wrapping and chilling. Make sure you allow the pastry to soften slightly before rolling.

• Lightly dust a work surface with flour.

• To prevent sticking, flour your hands and the rolling pin rather than showering the pastry with extra flour – this will avoid a build-up of powdery flour on the pastry.

• When rolling pastry, keep it moving on a 'hovercraft' of flour and it will never stick. Or try rolling pastry directly onto a piece of non-stick baking parchment or clingfilm/plastic wrap – this allows it be moved around easily and it will not stick to the work surface. The pastry can also be easily lifted and laid over a pie or tart without it stretching.

• Hold the rolling pin at either end, place on the pastry dough and always roll directly away from you. Move the pastry around by short turns in one direction so that you roll it evenly. Never flip the pastry over.

• Keep the rolling pin level for even thickness. Setting two chopsticks (or similar) on either side of the dough before rolling will help you to roll it out evenly to the thickness of the chopstick.

• Place your tart pan or pie dish on top of the rolled-out pastry to check it is large enough to cover the surface. Don't forget to include the height of the sides in your calculations.

• Once the pastry is the right size and thickness, roll the flour-dusted pastry around the rolling pin to help you to pick it up – this will avoid stretching the pastry and stop it shrinking when cooking.

LINING A TART PAN OR PIE DISH
• Drape the pastry over the pan and work it into the corners, being careful not to tear the pastry. (There is no need to grease a pan before lining, unless you have a vertical surface that you want the pastry to adhere to i.e. a deep loaf pan.)

• Use a small piece of extra pastry wrapped in a piece of clingfilm/plastic wrap to help to push the pastry into the edges of the pan.

• To make a single-crust pie, press the pastry up the sides of the pan and cut off the overhang with a very sharp knife. Or use a rolling pin to roll over the top, which will trim off any excess pastry very

neatly. (Don't trim the excess if making a doublecrust pie – you will trim both crusts off together.) Chill or freeze before baking.

BAKING BLIND

By 'baking blind', you pre-cook the pastry case so that it cooks through before the filling goes in and is less likely to become soggy. It also stops the pastry edges from collapsing into the filling.

• Prick the pastry all over with a fork.

• Line the pastry case with a piece of well-crumpled baking parchment or kitchen foil and fill with a layer of baking beans.

• Bake the pastry at 200°C (400°F) Gas 6 for 15 minutes then remove from the oven and lift out the baking parchment or foil and baking beans. Return to the oven and bake for a further

10 minutes or so until dried out, lightly golden and cooked through. Leave to cool.

FILLING A PIE

• Once the pan is lined, spoon in the cold filling, being careful not to splash the edges or overfill so that the top will seal properly.

• If the filling is likely to collapse slightly as it cooks (this will happen if raw fruit or meat is put in the pie), insert a pie funnel before you add the pastry lid. This will help steam escape as well as holding the pastry up so it cooks evenly and doesn't collapse into the dish. This is particularly important when putting a single-crust lid onto a deep-dish pie – the pastry can easily slip off the edges and collapse into the filling.

• Cover and cook as soon as possible.

Pâte sablée

This is a rich, sweet shortcrust but made with icing/confectioners' sugar to achieve a really lovely crisp, crumbly texture ('sablée' means sandy) that works perfectly with rich cream and fresh summer fruits.

200 g/1¾ sticks butter, softened
100 g/¾ cup icing/confectioners' sugar
a pinch of salt
1 vanilla pod/bean
finely grated zest of 1 lemon
2 eggs, lightly beaten
250 g/2 cups plain/all-purpose flour

**MAKES ENOUGH TO LINE
A 20-CM/8-IN. TART PAN**

Beat the butter, sugar and salt together in a stand mixer or in a bowl with an electric whisk until pale – about 5 minutes.

Split the vanilla bean lengthwise using a small, sharp knife and scrape the seeds out into the creamed butter mixture. Add the lemon zest and beat again to incorporate.

With the whisk running, gradually add the eggs, mixing until fully incorporated.

Gently mix in the flour but do not over-work the dough otherwise the gluten will develop and you will end up with pastry that is tough rather than crisp and light.

Bring the dough together into a ball with your hands, wrap in clingfilm/plastic wrap and refrigerate until needed – at least 2 hours, but overnight if possible.

Pâte sucrée

This is similar to the pâte sablée but the use of caster/superfine sugar instead of icing/confectioners' sugar makes a less delicate pastry. Use it to make tarts and as the base for gâteaux.

100 g/7 tablespoons butter, softened
100 g/1 cup caster/superfine sugar
1 vanilla pod/bean
finely grated zest of 1 lemon
2 eggs, lightly beaten
250 g/2 cups plain/all-purpose flour

**MAKES ENOUGH TO LINE
A 20-CM/8-IN. TART PAN**

Beat the butter and sugar together in a stand mixer or in a bowl with an electric whisk until pale – about 5 minutes.

Split the vanilla bean lengthwise using a small, sharp knife and scrape the seeds out into the creamed butter mixture. Add the lemon zest and beat again to incorporate.

With the whisk running, gradually add the eggs, mixing until fully incorporated.

Gently mix in the flour but do not over-work the dough otherwise the gluten will develop and you will end up with pastry that is tough rather than crisp and light.

Bring the dough together into a ball with your hands, wrap in clingfilm/plastic wrap and refrigerate until needed – at least 2 hours, but overnight if possible.

A

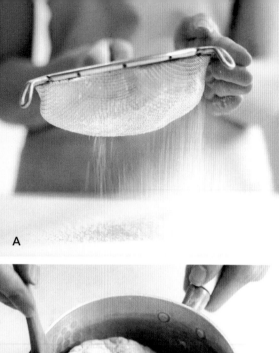

B

C

D

E

F

Basic choux pastry

This basic choux recipe needs a good strong arm – it is better beaten by hand than in a mixer as it is important to feel when the dough it ready. Unlike shortcrust and puff pastry, choux has a high moisture content as it contains water and lots of eggs. It is this moisture which causes the sticky choux paste to puff up into delicate pastry shells. It is important to weigh your ingredients accurately and to sift as much air into the flour for best results. The pastry can be made with water only, or a mixture of milk and water.

65 g/½ cup plain/all-purpose flour
50 g/3½ tablespoons butter, diced
75 ml/⅓ cup milk and 75 ml/⅓ cup water
    or 150 ml/⅔ cup water
1 teaspoon caster/superfine sugar
a pinch of salt
2 large eggs

MAKES 1 SINGLE QUANTITY

Some of the recipes in this book call for more than one quantity of pastry. Make in batches of no more than two quantities.

Sift the flour onto a sheet of baking parchment twice to remove any lumps and to add as much air as possible. (A)

Heat the butter in a saucepan with the milk and water (or just water if preferred), sugar and salt until the butter is melted. As soon as the butter is melted remove the pan from the heat and quickly shoot the sifted flour in all in one go. It is important not to let the water heat for longer than it takes to melt the butter as this will evaporate some of the water and so there will be less liquid for the pastry. (B)

Beat the mixture very hard with a wooden spoon or whisk until the dough forms a ball and no longer sticks to the sides of the pan and the pan is clean. At first the mixture will seem very wet but don't worry as it will come together after few minutes once the flour absorbs the water. It is important to really beat the mixture well at this stage. Leave to cool for about 5 minutes. (C)

Whisk the eggs in a separate bowl and then beat a small amount at a time into the pastry using a wooden spoon or a balloon whisk. The mixture will form a sticky paste which holds its shape when you lift the whisk up. When you first add the eggs and begin beating the mixture will split slightly. This is normal and the pastry will come back together as you continue to beat. The mixture must be beaten hard at each stage. (D) (E)

If the mixture is runny and does not hold its shape, unfortunately it cannot be used as it will not rise. Adding more flour to the mixture will not work. If this happens, unfortunately you will need to start again. (F)

Use the pastry following the steps in each recipe.

Crème pâtissière

This is without question the most luxurious cream on the planet! The basis of so many classic French pastries, this is rich, sweet, smooth and velvety.

1 vanilla pod/bean
500 ml/2 cups milk
100 g/½ cup raw cane sugar
4 egg yolks
3 tablespoons cornflour/cornstarch
3 tablespoons custard powder/vanilla pudding mix (or additional cornflour/cornstarch)
30 g/2 tablespoons butter

MAKES ABOUT 750 G/1½ LBS.

Split the vanilla pod lengthways using a small, sharp knife and scrape the seeds out into a large saucepan. Drop the bean in too and pour in the milk. Bring to the boil over low heat.

Meanwhile, in a mixing bowl, whisk the sugar, egg yolks, cornflour/cornstarch and custard powder together with a balloon whisk until smooth and creamy.

Pour half the boiled milk into the mixing bowl containing the egg mixture and whisk together. Now pour the contents of the bowl into the saucepan where the remaining milk is. Fish out the vanilla pod with a slotted spoon.

Over low heat, whisk the mixture until it thickens and starts to bubble. After 5 minutes, the heat will have cooked the cornflour and custard powder and become thick and rich.

Finally, add the butter and whisk it in until melted to further enrich the crème and make it extra glossy.

Transfer the crème pâtissière to a bowl and immediately place a sheet of clingfilm/plastic wrap over the surface to prevent a skin from forming. Allow to cool completely before using.

VARIATIONS

Chocolate: replace the cornflour/cornstarch and custard powder with 3½ teaspoons cornflour, 3 tablespoons plain/all-purpose flour and 3½ teaspoons cocoa powder. Follow the recipe as above, adding the cocoa powder at the same time as the cornflour. At the end, stir in 25 g/1 oz. melted dark/bittersweet chocolate.

Mango and passionfruit: replace the milk with a mixture of mango and passionfruit purées, or a combined mango and passionfruit smoothie.

Praline: add 50 g/¼ cup praline paste (available online) to the milk.

Boozy: stir in 1 tablespoon rum or Grand Marnier at the end.

Crème Chantilly

Almost everyone's idea of heaven, this is the simplest cream but it gives such joy and harmony to desserts. Spooned lovingly onto summer strawberries with a light grating of orange zest, or served as an accompaniment to a slice of rich, dense chocolate tart to help it go down, you need only four ingredients!

1 vanilla pod/bean
250 ml/1 cup whipping cream
250 ml/1 cup double/heavy cream
50 g/¼ cup caster/superfine sugar

MAKES ABOUT 550 G/1¼ LBS.

Split the vanilla pod lengthways using a small, sharp knife and scrape the seeds out into a stand mixer or use a mixing bowl and an electric whisk.

Add the whipping cream, double/heavy cream and sugar and beat until soft, billowing peaks form.

Be careful not to over-whip it otherwise it will become thick and grainy and won't be pleasant to eat – you want this cream to be luxuriously smooth and velvety.

Crème diplomate

Sometimes crème pâtissière can be too thick or rich for a delicate dessert pastry, so this cream is perfect.

250 ml/1 cup whipping cream
250 ml/1 cup double/heavy cream
500 g/2 cups store-bought crème pâtissière,
  or 1 quantity Crème Pâtissière (see opposite)

MAKES ABOUT 1 KG/2¼ LBS.

Put the whipping cream and double/heavy cream in a stand mixer or use a mixing bowl and an electric whisk. Beat until soft, billowing peaks form. Be careful not to over-whip it otherwise it will become thick and grainy and it will split when mixed in with the crème pâtissière.

Gently fold the whipped cream, in stages, into the crème pâtissière until smooth and irresistible. Refrigerate until ready to use (or eat straight from the bowl!).

Frangipane

Frangipane is so versatile that it can be used as a filling but equally it can be baked in a little cake pan and eaten as a delicious almond cake with a little jam/jelly and a cup of rich coffee.

100 g/7 tablespoons butter, softened
100 g/½ cup caster/superfine sugar
3 eggs
100 g/1 cup ground almonds
2½ tablespoons plain/all-purpose flour

MAKES ABOUT 400 G/14 OZ.

Beat the butter and sugar together in a stand mixer or in a bowl with an electric whisk on high speed for up to 4 minutes. You don't want to get too much air in there otherwise it will puff up in the oven – frangipane should be dense and moist.

Add the eggs, one at a time, and beat until well mixed.

Fold in the ground almonds and flour with a large spoon until evenly incorporated.

The frangipane will keep in an airtight container in the fridge for a few days.

Lemon curd

Lemon curd is one of the easiest things to make, and can form the base of all manner of summer soufflés, ice creams, and fillers for cakes and tarts.

5 eggs
150 g/¾ cup caster/superfine sugar
grated zest and juice of 3 large lemons
  or 125 ml/½ cup lemon juice
175 g/1½ sticks butter, softened and diced

MAKES ENOUGH TO FILL 10 SMALL TARTLETS OR 1 LARGE TART

Place the eggs, caster sugar, lemon zest and juice in a heatproof bowl set over a pan one-third filled with water. Bring to the boil over medium–high heat, then reduce to a simmer.

Whisk for about 8 minutes over the heat until the sugar has dissolved and the mixture has thickened.

Add the cubes of butter, one at a time, and whisk until smooth, then remove from the heat. Set the lemon curd aside to cool.

Italian meringue

This type of meringue is generally used for topping tarts or pies and then coloured with the heat of a blowtorch.

125 g/scant ⅔ cup caster/superfine sugar
2 egg whites, at room temperature
a pinch of cream of tartar
a pinch of salt

sugar thermometer
kitchen blowtorch

MAKES ENOUGH TO TOP 12 SMALL TARTLETS OR 1 LARGE TART

Tip the sugar into a small pan and add 75 ml/ 5 tablespoons of water. Set the pan over low heat. Once the sugar is dissolved, bring to the boil and pop a sugar thermometer into the pan.

Meanwhile, tip the egg whites into the bowl of a stand mixer fitted with a whisk attachment and add the cream of tartar and salt.

Continue to cook the syrup until it reaches 110°C (230°F) on the thermometer. Then start whisking the egg whites until they will hold soft, floppy peaks. Remove the syrup from the heat, and with the mixer running on a medium speed, steadily pour into the egg whites being careful to not let the syrup hit the whisk, otherwise it will simply splatter against the sides of the bowl. Increase the speed and continue whisking for a further 4–5 minutes until the meringue is cool, stiff and glossy.

Working quickly either spoon the meringue on top of the individual or large tart you are making or fill a piping/pastry bag and pipe peaks on top. Light the blowtorch and lightly scorch the meringue. Leave to cool before serving.

Index

Recipe credits

VALERIE AIKMAN-SMITH
Lemon Curd Tartlets with
    Rhubarb & Ginger

BRONTE AURELL
Apricot Tart with Mazarin
Gooseberry Pavlova
Napoleon Cakes
Raspberry Squares
Summer Berry Tart

MAXINE CLARK
Free-form Caramelized
    Peach Tart
Lattice-topped Cherry Pie
Pineapple & Passion Curd
    Tartlets

JULIAN DAY
Rhubarb & Mascarpone Tart

URSULA FERRIGNO
Lemon, Cardamom &
    Raspberry Torte
Lemon Profiteroles

MAT FOLLAS
Lemon & Lime Meringue Tartlets
Rhubarb & Custard Slice
Summer Fruit Jam Tarts

LIZ FRANKLIN
Clotted Cream & Raspberry
    Brulée Tartlets
Fresh Apricot Tart

HANNAH MILES
Apricot Vanilla Tart
Blackcurrant Millefeuilles
Blueberry Pie
Blueberry & Lemon Drizzle
    Cakes
Caramelized Tartes au Citron
Cherry Pie

Individual Plum Tartes Tatin
Fresh Fruit Eclairs
Glazed French Fruit Tart
Glazed Mango Mousse Pie
Gluten-free Nectarine & Cream
    Choux Rings
Gluten-free Strawberry Tartlets
Key Lime Pie
Lemon Meringue Choux Buns
Lemon & Raspberry Roulade
Lime Charlotte Cake
Mini Citrus Meringue Pies
Passion Fruit Eclairs
Peaches & Cream Choux Rings
    with Amaretti Crumble
    Topping
Peach Melba Meringue Layer
Pile-high Peach Pie
Pina Colada Pie
Pineapple & Coconut
    Millefeuilles
Pineapple & Star Anise Tartes
    Tatin
Puff Pastry Strawberry Ring
Raspberry Chiffon Layer Cake
Raspberry & Rose Tartlets
Rose & Raspberry Choux Rings
Rustic Plum Tart
Strawberry Choux Ring
Strawberry Layer Cake with
    Chantilly Cream
Summer Berry Tartlets
Tarte au Citron
White Chocolate & Lavender
    Profiteroles

MIISA MINK
Blueberry Tart with Rye
Rhubarb Meringue Pie
Rhubarb Tart
Summer Berry Lattice Tart

WILL TORRENT
Cherry & Almond Bakewell tarts
Chocolate & Cherry Tarts

Mango & Coconut Millefeuilles
Mango & Passion Fruit Mini
    Eclairs
Passion Fruit Meringue Tarts
Plum Pithiviers
Raspberry & Rose Millefeuilles
Strawberry & Champagne Tarts
Strawberry & Pistachio Tartlets
Tarte Exotique

LAURA WASHBURN HUTTON
Fresh Fruit Tart

BEA VO
Green Tea Cream Tart with
    Strawberries

Photography credits